GLORIA'S GOURMET LOW-FAT MUFFINS

D0959589

GLORIA AMBROSIA

Avery Publishing Group
Garden City Park, New York

Cover Designer: William Gonzalez
Text Illustrator: John Wincek
In-House Editor: Marie Caratozzolo
Typesetters: William Gonzalez and Nuno Faisca
Printer: Paragon Press, Honesdale, PA

Library of Congress Cataloging-in-Publication Data

Ambrosia, Gloria.
    Gloria's gourmet low-fat muffins / Gloria Ambrosia.
       p. cm.
    Includes index.
    ISBN 0-89529-732-9
    1. Muffins.   2. Low-fat diet–Recipes.   I. Title.
TX770.M83A46 1996
641.8'15–dc20   96-27164
                                          CIP

Printed in the United States of America
10 9 8 7 6 5 4 3 2 1

CONTENTS

ACKNOWLEDGMENTS

A book like this doesn't come about without a lot of help from family and friends. I want to express a very special thanks to Boyce and Janet at Friends of the Earth natural foods store in Winston-Salem, North Carolina. They have always been extremely generous with their expertise on matters of health, nutrition, and natural foods products. They have encouraged my efforts from day one, and have sold hundreds of dozens of my creations—enjoying more than a few dozen themselves, I expect!

An extra special thanks to Patty McGann for encouraging me throughout and for giving me a fantastic place to live while I wrote much of this book; and to her dog Sascha for guarding the stove while my muffins baked and for taste testing just about every batch.

Special thanks to Douglas, Susan and George Wolff, and to Astra Stroebel for letting me test my muffins in their fabulous kitchens while my own kitchen underwent reorganization. And to my oldest, dearest friend Nancy Rickenbach for listening to me chatter about the book for hours, for testing many of my recipes, and for giving me feedback.

Thanks to my mom and sisters and nieces and nephews and Donna and Cashin and Barbara and Gwen for their encouragement.

And thanks to Marie and the folks at Avery Publishing Group for helping make the entire experience an absolute joy.

PREFACE

"Speaking off the record, after baking hundreds of dozens of muffins in order to write your cookbook, aren't you just a little bit tired and glad that the book is done?" asked the reporter from my local newspaper. She was interviewing me following the publication of my first muffin cookbook, *Gloria's Glorious Muffins*. Earlier in the interview she had asked how I came to write the book. Had I conducted a comprehensive analysis of the cookbook market and discovered an obvious niche? Was I looking for a quick and easy way to make a buck? Was I a baker by profession?

I recall being amused by her questions because I knew I had neither gimmicks nor insider information about what was hot and what was not in cookbooks (I'm not that sophisticated!). And anyone who has ever written a cookbook knows that it involves a tremendous amount of work and is, for the majority of authors, not all that profitable.

The simple truth about *Gloria's Glorious Muffins* is that it grew out of my wish to make a living doing the things I like best—being creative in the kitchen, sharing my creations with others, and writing about the tales that go with these activities. That's all there was to it.

"No. I am not tired of the process," I answered the reporter. "To tell you the truth, I'm sorry it's over." I was thinking about how much more there was to learn about muffins, how many recipes and ideas were still spinning around in my head, and how I might even like to write another muffin cookbook. Little did I know that three years and hundreds of baking hours later, that's just what I would do.

Gloria's Gourmet Low-Fat Muffins is a collection of my best muffins yet. I created these recipes to accommodate the sensible eating trends of our times.

As you will see, I use ingredients that are wholesome and nutritious—the kinds of ingredients that you can feel good about eating. What is more, I've managed to keep the fat content of my muffins very low. Nearly all the muffins in this book contain less than 3 grams of fat and derive less than 15 percent of their calories from fat. All this without compromising flavor! In fact, I think you will find these muffins to be some of the most delicious you have ever eaten.

I have also worked hard to make sure that my muffins are quick and easy to bake. Muffins should be simple affairs. Don't you think so? You shouldn't have to scour the countryside searching for ingredients that you've either never heard of or aren't sure you want to use. And you shouldn't have to spend hours in the kitchen to make muffins that turn out right.

Finally, use of the software program, DINE Healthy, by DINE Systems, Inc., has made it possible for me to offer you precise nutritional information with every recipe. You will know *exactly* what you are eating.

Gloria's Gourmet Low-Fat Muffins begins with an extensive introductory chapter entitled "Helpful Hints and Information." Here, you will find important information on the ingredients, tools, and techniques that are important for successful muffin-making. Nutritional information is also included in this chapter.

Subsequent chapters include a variety of flavorful and nutritious muffin recipes. Enjoy the "Fresh & Fruity, Sometimes Nutty, Anytime Muffins" at any time of the day or night. "Crunchy, Crumbly, Spicy Do-Da Muffins" are just right with coffee and tea. And the "Herby Cheesy Muffin Thangs" are perfect accompaniments to salads and dinner entrées. I created the "Chocolate Every-Which-Way-But-Fat Muffins" for the chocolate-lovers in your life. A variety of luscious toppings and glazes crown many of the "Over-the-Top and Out-of-the-Question Muffins," which are made with exotic ingredients. One thing is sure—no matter which chapter you turn to, you will find scrumptious low-fat muffins for every occasion—or for no occasion at all!

Throughout the book, I have offered educational tidbits on specific muffin ingredients and procedures, informative charts and tables, and a number of reflective passages that are designed to help you enjoy baking to the fullest. Finally, I have included a "Quick Reference Guide," which lists my muffins and their defining ingredients. This will save you from having to thumb through the entire book to select a muffin that includes a particular ingredient (or ingredients) you want.

I wrote *Gloria's Gourmet Low-Fat Muffins* for you. I truly hope you enjoy it.

INTRODUCTION

L ast Fourth of July, I met my friend John in Washington, D.C. He flew in from Los Angeles to participate in a square-dance convention and together we planned to take part in the Independence Day festivities and visit the national monuments. Washington has to be one of the most beautiful cities in the world, and it is especially breathtaking at that time of year.

After taking an early morning subway from the Omni Hotel, where we were staying, to the Ellipse, we spent the morning on foot visiting the White House, Lafayette Park, and various points of interest in that immediate area. Then John and I decided to walk the several-mile touring route around the Tidal Basin to visit the monuments.

Somewhere between the Washington Monument and the Jefferson Memorial my tootsies screamed for a rest. "How 'bout we find a comfy park bench, put our feet up, and feed the pigeons and squirrels for awhile?" I suggested. "Sounds good to me," was John's reply.

As we made our way to an inviting area of the park just on the edge of the Tidal Basin, we passed an enchanting little refreshment stand—colorful, festive, scalloped umbrella, the whole bit—whose menu included so-called wholesome snacks. I selected a fruit drink and a lemon-blueberry muffin. John chose banana nut.

As we sat feeling the warmth of friendship and the satisfaction of a delightful morning, I glanced at the nutrition label on the muffin wrapper I was about to toss into a nearby bin. Fat: 32 grams. I said, "32 grams! This is a wholesome snack? You've got to be kidding! That's more fat than I want to eat all day!" John's muffin contained the same amount of fat. He agreed it was indecent and, without a flicker, we wrapped up the remains of our muffins and tossed them into the bin. Bummer. You know what I mean? Bummer. Baking muffins as often as I do, I know that it's easy to make delicious varieties without much fat. And even a light sprinkling of nuts won't balloon the fat content to 32 grams!

What John and I discovered is not uncommon. Many muffins packaged for commercial sale contain inordinate amounts of fat. It's as if the manufacturers think that fat enhances the flavor of foods. It doesn't. Fat actually deadens the flavor. It's like so many gobs of goo coating our taste buds and obstructing the ability to taste the true flavors of the foods we eat. The natural flavor of a low-fat muffin is rich. And we can turn to natural ingredients such as spices, fruit, and citrus rind to wake up these wonderful flavors even more.

Today you can buy a number of commercial low-fat muffin products, and some of them are pretty good. But my enthusiasm for such products usually sinks when I read the list of ingredients. Chemical additives, typically used for coloring, flavoring, or extending product shelf life, are usually included. If I can't pronounce the ingredients on the label, I don't eat the contents therein.

When it comes down to it, I'd rather make my own muffins. They are so quick and easy to bake. Even if the need arises suddenly, I can make a batch of muffins from start to finish in twenty to thirty minutes. Or I can turn to the freezer, where I always have a few dozen on hand.

Muffins are about as perfect as food can be. I mean, how often do you find a basic food item that is not only wholesome and nutritious but also delicious, heart-healthy, immensely satisfying, and suitable for enjoying any time of the day? Baking muffins is also an enjoyable, pleasant, creative experience—and one of the nicest things we can do for ourselves and the people we love.

1.

HELPFUL HINTS & INFORMATION

Making muffins, with all of their attractive qualities, is simply a matter of gathering together the proper ingredients, then preparing and combining them in such a way as to ensure success. (Of course, you also need fabulous recipes—which is why I wrote this book!) This chapter is intended to take the guesswork out of the muffin-making process and help you to become a fabulous muffin baker.

INGREDIENTS

I've taken measures to create muffin recipes that call for wholesome and nutritious ingredients that are readily available at your local grocery and health food stores. These days one-stop shopping is possible in most cities and towns because more and more commercial grocery stores are carrying products that were once available only in health food and specialty food shops. Some stores devote entire aisles to such items. When you shop, you should have no trouble finding the ingredients needed to make *Gloria's Gourmet Low-Fat Muffins*.

I like to keep a basic supply of muffin ingredients on hand at all times. This is not difficult because most of the ingredients store easily and for long periods of time. I have designated a cupboard and a special corner in my refrigerator for muffin ingredients, and I try to keep these areas well stocked. Then, whenever the urge hits me, I can bake just about any muffin in my repertoire. Here is my list of muffin-making staples:

- Baking powder
- Baking soda
- Bran: oat and wheat
- Chocolate: milk chocolate and semi-sweet chips
- Cocoa powder
- Coconut (flaked)
- Cornmeal: blue, white, and/or yellow
- Dairy products: nonfat buttermilk, skim milk, nonfat sour cream, nonfat cream cheese
- Dried fruits: apricots, currants, prunes, raisins
- Eggs
- Extracts: almond, rum, strawberry, vanilla
- Flours: brown rice, buckwheat, oat, rye, soy, unbleached white, whole-wheat, whole-wheat pastry
- Granola, low-fat
- Lemon and orange peel
- Margarine, light
- Nuts: almonds, pecans, walnuts
- Oats, rolled
- Oils: canola, olive
- Salt
- Sweeteners: apple- and orange-juice concentrates, applesauce, light brown and dark brown sugars, fresh fruit, honey, maple syrup, molasses
- Wheat germ, toasted

What follows in this section is a listing of the ingredients I use most often and a few things I would like you to know about them.

FLOUR

The principal ingredient in muffins is flour. You may notice that my recipes call for a variety of flours. For most muffins, I use whole-wheat, whole-wheat pastry, and unbleached white flours because they are most readily available, and I want to make muffin-baking as easy as possible for you. I am also fond of barley, brown rice, buckwheat, rye, and soy flours, as well as cornmeal and rolled oats. These add flavor and nutritional variety to muffins.

Whole-Wheat Flour

Whenever I eat cooked wheat berries I understand why wheat, in its many forms, is consumed in larger quantities worldwide than any other cereal grain. The cooked berry is hearty, chewy, and satisfying to the taste, and I can actually feel the wholesome goodness going to work on my body making it strong and healthy.

Whole-wheat is high in protein, fiber, and complex carbohydrates. It also contains vitamin E and several important B vitamins. But in order to get the full benefits from wheat, one must eat the whole wheat berry—including the bran (the outer layer, which constitutes about 14 percent of the total weight of the wheat kernel), the wheat germ (the embryo or seed, which makes up about 3 percent of the weight), and the endosperms (the starchy middle part, which comprises 83 percent of the weight of the kernel).

Whole-wheat flour is just that—the whole-wheat berry that has been milled into a fine powder. All of the nutritional components of the whole-wheat kernel are intact. Highly processed flour, on the other hand, contains only the endosperms, the part with the least nutritional value. When buying whole-wheat flour, make certain the package says 100 percent whole-wheat. This means that the flour has been made from the whole-wheat berry and nothing has been processed out.

Whole-Wheat Pastry Flour

Whole-wheat pastry flour is made from soft red winter wheat, not the hard winter wheat that is used to make whole-wheat flour. It is still whole-wheat flour in that it has been milled from the whole-wheat berry, but whole-wheat pastry flour is lighter. A cup of whole-wheat flour weighs 113 grams; a cup of whole-wheat pastry flour, 90 grams. Whole-wheat pastry flour also contains less protein than hard winter wheat flour—7 to 10 percent protein as compared to 12 to 15 percent.

One might think that the lightness of whole-wheat pastry flour would make it a more desirable choice for muffins than regular whole-wheat flour. But the lightness of the flour doesn't necessarily mean that muffins will be lighter. In fact, it is the presence of protein in wheat that makes the batter rise during baking; and whole-wheat pastry flour contains less protein than regular whole-wheat flour. I've noticed that if I use only whole-wheat pastry flour in a muffin recipe, the muffins are not as successful as when I also add whole-wheat flour.

Whole-wheat pastry flour does not absorb moisture in the same way as other flours. Thus, it is only interchangeable with other flours up to about ¼ to ⅓ cup. Beyond that amount, you must reduce the amount of liquid in the recipe. You can substitute whole-wheat pastry flour with equal amounts of regular whole wheat and unbleached white flour.

Unbleached White Flour

In my first muffin cookbook, I shied away from using too much unbleached white flour thinking it was less desirable than the whole-wheat variety. I've since warmed up to it. While it's true that unbleached white flour contains less fiber than its less-refined parent product, it also contains less fat — a desirable feature for our purposes. Besides, we can easily compensate for the comparatively weaker nutritional makeup of unbleached white flour by using it in combination with whole-wheat flour or by adding wheat or oat bran to balance things out.

You may be interested to know that there are brands of unbleached white flour available at your local health food store that retain some of the bran and germ. These are usually labeled as whole-grain white flours.

Barley Flour

I have a theory that if we paid closer attention to the flavor of the foods we eat, we would quite naturally eat what is good for us. Barley is a good example. This grain is so delicious and so satisfying that sometimes I cook up a big bowl of whole-grain barley and eat it all by itself. Mmm. And I don't want to eat anything else with it—except maybe a dash of soy sauce.

I have come to find out that barley has lots of cholesterol-lowering fiber—more than six times the amount found in brown rice and unbleached white flours and twice that in rye and whole-wheat pastry flours (*see* Table 1.1 Nutrient Analysis of Flours, Cornmeal, and Oats found on pages 8–9). Besides, barley is more easily digested than wheat, which is why it is often used in baby food. When our digestive system is operating properly, we tend to be bright and alert.

The trouble is, in order to enjoy the beneficial properties from this grain, we must eat it in its whole-grain form. Unfortunately, most commercially available barley and barley flour has been processed to remove the outer hull. "Pearling," as the process is called, destroys almost all of the fiber in barley and about half of its nutrients. Flour made from unhulled barley is available at many health-food stores. If your local store doesn't carry it, ask the manager if he or she would be willing to order it for you.

Brown Rice Flour

Brown rice flour is made from hulled whole-grain rice—rice that has been processed to remove the outer hull. Like barley flour, brown rice flour is sweet to the taste, making it an ideal muffin ingredient. This grain derives its sweetness from an abundance of complex carbohydrates—132 grams per cup of flour compared to 80 grams per cup of whole-wheat flour and 67 grams per cup of whole-wheat pastry flour. Complex carbohydrates, with their slow, steady digestibility, are the best source of energy for our bodies. Muffins made with brown rice flour are like the Eveready Energizer battery. They help us keep going and going and going.

Buckwheat Flour

As I wrote in my first book, there are two kinds of people in the world—those who like buckwheat and those who don't. I'm one of the former. I like the way its strong nutty flavor dominates a muffin and gives it that special taste. In addition to having a distinctive flavor, buckwheat is high in protein and fiber. It is also very high in potassium, a nutrient necessary to regulate the heartbeat and maintain proper fluid balance and blood pressure.

Table 1.1 Nutrient Analysis of Flours, Cornmeal, and Oats

The nutritional breakdown of the following is based on 1-cup servings.

Product	Calories	Fat gms	Chol. mgs	Protein gms
Barley Flour	400	2	0	14
Brown Rice Flour	600	3	0	12
Buckwheat Flour	400	4	0	16
Cornmeal, White	434	4	0	10
Cornmeal, Yellow	434	4	0	10
Oats, Rolled	300	6	0	10
Rye Flour	400	2	0	12
Soy Flour	400	18	0	32
White Flour (unbleached)	400	1	0	12
Whole-Wheat Flour	400	2	0	15
Whole-Wheat Pastry Flour	303	2	0	10

Buckwheat flour comes in two varieties: light and dark. Light buckwheat flour is usually made from the whole seed minus the hard outer shell, while the dark variety contains both the seed and most of its hull. Dark buckwheat flour is the more nutritious of the two. In fact, it contains more protein per measure than any other grain. (Actually, buckwheat is not wheat at all; in fact, it's not even a grain. It's the seed of an herb!) If the flour has dark flecks that look something like the vanilla bean flecks found in better ice creams, you'll know you have the dark buckwheat flour. Buy it. It'll knock your socks off.

Cornmeal

What I said about barley can also be said about cornmeal. It's the good tasting things in life that are often the best for us. Cornmeal is an excellent source of fiber and complex carbohydrates. Its sweet, nutty flavor makes it a popular ingredient for muffins.

Always purchase cornmeal that has been stone-ground or water-ground.

Fiber gms	Carbs gms	Sodium mgs	Calcium mgs	Iron mgs	Potas. gms
19.4	86	4	20	1.8	182
3.0	132	15	60	3.2	393
12.0	84	0	0	4.3	70
8.8	92	42	7	4.2	344
8.8	92	42	7	4.2	344
8.0	54	0	0	3.6	280
9.7	83	0	20	4.5	230
16.0	32	0	160	9.0	1500
3.4	86	0	0	4.5	140
13.0	80	10	20	3.6	420
9.1	67	0	61	3.3	348

Unlike other milling processes for corn, these grinding techniques do not re-move the hull and germ—the most nutritious parts of the corn kernel. And milling corn in this way diminishes the likelihood that muffins made with cornmeal will crumble to bits when you slice or bite into them. (You know, the way some cornmeal muffins do!)

Rolled Oats, Oat Flour, and Oat Bran

Reasons abound for using rolled oats, oat flour, and oat bran in muffins. For one thing, these products have a sweet and pleasing flavor. (What can I say? I always seem to weigh that factor first.) They contain a natural antioxidant that helps to keep muffins moist, reducing the need for fat or oil. A good source of carbohydrates, protein, B vitamins, and minerals, oats are also con-sidered to be one of the most nutritionally complete of all grains. But perhaps most important, there has been a considerable amount of research linking the consumption of oats, particularly oat bran, with low cholesterol levels. It is believed that cholesterol sticks to the soluble fiber in oat bran and is thereby flushed out of the body easily.

What distinguishes rolled oats from oat flour and oat bran? Oats are commonly prepared by flattening the whole grain or groat into a disk. Rolling, as this process is called, makes the oats easier to cook without robbing the grain of its nutritional value. Oats can also be milled into flour for use in baking. During the milling process, the bran can be removed from the oats and packaged separately. Look for oat bran among the hot cereals in your grocery store.

Rye Flour

Rye flour, which is quite popular, can be found in most grocery stores next to the whole-wheat flours and cornmeals. Surprisingly high in fiber, rye flour contains three times the fiber found in brown rice flour and unbleached white flour, and a tad more than that found in whole-wheat pastry flour. Read the label when selecting rye flour. Most commercial brands are primarily wheat. Check the list of ingredients to be sure that the product contains only rye flour or that the rye is listed first among the ingredients. It is also important to know that, like other types of flour, rye is milled in several ways. Dark rye flour is made from whole rye berries and has the nutrition of whole-grain rye intact. The package usually reads "whole-grain" rye flour. Light and medium rye flours, however, have had the bran and/or germ removed, which means much of the nutritional value is gone.

Soy Flour

The appeal of soy flour is its nutritional value. While it contains much more fat per measure than any other flour (18 grams of fat per cup compared to 2 grams in whole-wheat flour), it also contains more than twice the protein of most other flours and nearly twice the fiber.

I suppose I'd use soy flour more liberally than I do if it weren't for two things: It is pungent and bitter-tasting, and it is surprisingly heavy. If you use too much of it in muffins, they come out dense and flat. Not at all desirable. So I use soy flour only in those muffins that I feel could use a little protein boost, and I use only 2 to 4 tablespoons per batch of muffins. Some soy flours have been treated or slightly toasted for improved flavor and digestibility.

RISING AGENTS

Did you ever notice that some muffins rise more than others? Me, too. In my early days of muffin-making I drove myself crazy trying to make all of my muffins the same size and shape. I finally realized it was impossible. Muffins are like people. They come in all shapes and sizes. Different combinations of ingredients produce different-shaped muffin products. That's all there is to it. Muffins with heavier, denser ingredients such as whole-wheat flour, dried fruits, or fruit purées are going to be slightly heavier and denser than those made with lighter flours. Likewise, muffins made with ingredients such as nonfat sour cream or nonfat yogurt always seems to sit taller in the saddle. That's part of what makes muffins so interesting.

Having said that, I must add that you can optimize the rising action of your muffins by selecting the right rising agent for the job. The idea is to produce muffin batter that is not so acidic that it bubbles out of control before you even have a chance to put it in the oven, and not so alkaline that it has no oomph at all. Baking powder is a nicely balanced combination of acid power (cream of tartar) and alkaline power (bicarbonate of soda). It produces batter with the right kind of rising action. Because many of my batters contain such acidic ingredients as fruit purées, citrus juice, and honey, I balance the rising action by using baking soda in combination with the baking powder.

When buying rising agents, bear in mind that they do not have a long shelf life. If your muffins are consistently turning out flat and squat, it's probably because your rising agent is flat and squat. Throw it out and buy a fresh supply. If you bake infrequently, buy small packages.

If you ever run out of baking powder, don't worry. Mix cream of tartar and bicarbonate of soda, two-to-one, and measure the mixture as you would commercial baking powder. It is essentially the same thing.

SALT

Salt enhances the flavors in muffins. The trick is to select a pure salt product and not use too much of it.

What we commonly know as table salt is pure sodium chloride with added iodine. Because it is mined from inland deposits that are millions of years old, all the useful trace minerals have long since evaporated. In addition, regular table salt usually contains additives to make it more free-flowing. A better choice than regular table salt is a low-sodium salt product that contains 33 percent less sodium and is iodine-free. However, I believe an even better choice to be sea salt. High in trace minerals, sea salt is obtained from evaporated sea water. It contains no sugar or chemical additives.

Table salt. Low-sodium salt. Sea salt. Use whichever one makes sense to you. When I use salt in my muffins, it is in very small amounts—only one-quarter teaspoon per batch.

SWEETENERS

I never liked overly sweet muffins. There's a restaurant in my town that serves a walnut muffin that is so sweet I can taste the sugar on my lips long after I've taken a bite. Yuk! It's really not a muffin at all. It's a cupcake. I prefer the sweetness of my muffins to be more subtle than that.

To achieve the subtle sweet taste I like, I rely on the wholesome goodness of fresh fruit, fruit-juice concentrates, dried fruit, and fruit purées; the syrupy sweetness of honey, molasses and maple syrup; the robust flavor of light brown sugar; and occasionally, when I am trying to achieve a more dessert-like muffin, table sugar. I also use what I call my magic ingredients—spices, extracts, and citrus rind. These perk up the natural flavors of muffins and give the illusion of added sweetness.

Fresh Fruit

Many of my recipes call for fresh fruit—apples, ripe bananas, blueberries, dark sweet cherries, mangoes, peaches, pears, and raspberries. I like using fruit because, in addition to being high in complex carbohydrates—the energy nutrient—it is also high in fiber. And fruit is convenient to use. Fresh apples and bananas are available year round, while other fruits are always available either frozen or canned.

Fruit Juice and Fruit-Juice Concentrates

Fruit juice and fruit-juice concentrates give muffins a natural sweetness. However, I limit the use of these items because too much may cause the muffins to burn, often before they are fully cooked. I never use more than a half cup of fruit juice or a quarter cup of concentrate per batch of muffins.

When buying fruit juices and concentrates, check the ingredient label to make sure they do not contain added sugar. The natural products are sweet enough.

Dried Fruit

Dried fruits are great muffin sweeteners. They are particularly handy because, when properly stored, they have a long shelf life. Apples, apricots, dates, figs, grapes, peaches, pears, and plums are the most popular dried fruits. While these dried-fruit varieties are readily available in most grocery and health food stores, you may have to check specialty shops for the dried cranberries and raspberries that I use in some of my muffins. Trust me. It will be worth the effort.

Until recently, it seemed that one fruit-preserving company dominated the dried-fruit market. Recently, however, perhaps because of increased interest in dried fruit as a low-fat snack food, I have seen and sampled quality products from a number of lesser-known companies. This is good news for consumers, as it helps ensure competitive prices.

Fruit Purées

In the process of creating muffins for this cookbook, I discovered the value of prune purées, apple butter, and applesauce. These not only sweeten the pot but also moisten the batter, diminishing the need for fat or oil. According to one manufacturer of prune and apple butters, substituting purées for the shortening in baking reduces fat by 75 to 90 percent and calories by 20 to 30 percent. I have found this to be true.

Honey

Although honey is not much different chemically from table sugar (that is, it isn't particularly high in nutrition), there are four good reasons to use it instead of sugar whenever possible. (I made these same four points in my first muffin cookbook, but they merit repeating here.) First, honey is twice as sweet as refined sugar so we tend to use less. Second, honey adds moisture to muffins so we can use less fat. Third, honey's sweetness comes from sugars that are absorbed into the body more slowly than table sugar so they provide a steadier supply of energy. And, fourth, when purchased from noncommercial sources, honey is a natural and unprocessed food.

I buy honey from a local beekeeper who sells to markets around town and throughout the county. He takes a lot of pride in his bees and the honey they produce. An expert, he knows that the taste, color, and texture of the honey changes with the seasons according to what the bees are attracted to at the time. Buying from a local supplier such as this assures that the honey is fresh and unprocessed.

In my first muffin cookbook, I recommended warming the honey before mixing it with the other wet ingredients. Warming facilitates blending—especially when the honey is thick or when the wet ingredients are particularly cold. Over the years, however, I have found that buying fresh honey and storing it properly make warming an unnecessary step. Fresh honey maintains a syrupy consistency. Stored at room temperature, it is always easy to use.

Molasses

A friend of mine from the mountains of North Carolina says he was fifteen years old before he learned that the sweet brown syrup he poured all over his hot cereal and toast every morning was called "molasses" and not simply "lasses." That's because he and his seven brothers and sisters loved the syrup so much that it was constantly on the move around the breakfast table. "Can I please have some mow lasses," one or another of them would cry out with their thick Southern drawl. And the "lasses" would be sent on its way.

"Lasses" adds a certain gusto to the flavor of muffins. It is rich in energy-providing carbohydrates as well as iron and potassium—two nutrients that are especially good for the heart. You can buy molasses in a range of flavors and intensities—from regular (probably the most popular), to robust (the flavor I like best), to the thick and dark blackstrap molasses (too intense and too thick for our purposes).

Maple Syrup

Is the price of real maple syrup coming down or is it just that my grocer now stocks a less-expensive brand? I had grown so accustomed to paying four or five dollars for a pint of maple syrup that I would hardly bat an eye when I grabbed it off the shelf. For the past year or so, however, the price has been half that. Needless to say, the first time I noticed the lower price I checked the label to make sure the syrup was 100 percent pure maple. It was. I hope these lower prices are not a passing phenomenon.

There's nothing like real maple syrup, is there? Such a unique flavor. And so rich! Do you know that it takes up to fifty gallons of sap from maple trees to make only one gallon of syrup? Thanks maple trees.

Sugars, White and Brown

I used to believe that commercial brands of brown sugar were better than refined white sugar. However, except for the presence of a few trace elements, brown sugar is as low in nutritional value as white sugar. Now I use it not so much because I imagine it to be better, it's just that I like the flavor. What gives brown sugar its color and distinctive flavor is molasses, an ingredient that gives muffins pizzazz. If your palate does not agree, feel free to substitute white sugar for the brown in my recipes.

Spices, Extracts, and Citrus Peel

My last sweet secret is to incorporate aromatic spices, extracts, and flavorings, and the sweet zing of lemon and orange peel into my muffins. They have a way of making muffins taste light and sweet. (For information on preparing citrus peel, see page 21.)

EGGS AND EGG PRODUCTS

My main objective in writing *Gloria's Gourmet Low-Fat Muffins* was to create muffins that are low in fat without compromising flavor or texture. To do this I needed to address the egg question. So I experimented. I created muffins using the whole egg, egg whites only, and cholesterol-free and fat-free egg products. Then I compared the results. Here's what I found.

While there are a number fat- and cholesterol-free egg products in the commercial food market that may be attractive for one reason or another, I can't, in good conscience, recommend them for muffin making. For one thing, most of these products are egg whites with added coloring agents, thickeners, and preservatives. In other words, they are not really food as we have come to appreciate it. I can understand why people might use such products in French toast, quiches, scrambled "eggs," and dishes in which it is important to visually create the appearance of whole eggs. But this is not necessary for muffins. Why use a product with unwanted additives if we don't have to? Besides, I found that muffins made with such products tend to be tough and rubbery. I don't like that. Prepared egg products might be easy to use, but they do not yield muffins that meet my high standards.

One of the simplest ways to reduce the fat in muffins is to limit the use of whole eggs or to use only the whites. ("Don't bake until you add the whites of the eggs.") While I do not hesitate to state that you can feel free to use whole eggs and egg whites interchangeably (one whole egg is equal to two egg whites), there is no question that using only egg whites alters the texture of the final product. The difference, however, is nominal, and whipping the egg whites until they are nearly stiff before adding them to the batter diminishes that difference. (*See* Whip the Eggs First, If You Like on page 24.)

You may be wondering, if there's not much difference between egg whites and whole eggs as far as texture and consistency are concerned, why use the whole egg at all? Answer: Some recipes simply come out better with whole eggs. For example, I tend to use a whole egg in muffins with fruit or vegetable purées. The egg protein contained in the yolk seems to hold things together better. (But there are exceptions. For example, I use egg whites instead of the whole egg when the fat content of the muffins is right at the maximum standard of 3 grams, and using the whole egg would cause the recipe to exceed that standard.)

I found it interesting that using the whole egg does not appreciably affect the fat content of each muffin (the 5 grams of fat in one egg is divided between 10 to 12 muffins). It does, however, increase the cholesterol from 0 milligrams to about 18. The USDA recommends that our daily intake of cholesterol not exceed 300 milligrams (one egg contains about 220 milligrams). It is easy to see that at 18 to 20 milligrams of cholesterol per muffin, one can eat quite a few before exceeding the limit.

If you are on an egg-free diet, you may consider using cornstarch as an egg substitute. Two tablespoons of cornstarch sifted together with the dry ingredients behaves like one whole egg.

SHORTENING

Nearly all my muffins contain less than 3 grams of fat. This is possible by keeping a tight rein on shortening. You will notice that while many of my muffins contain no oil at all, those that do, contain only one tablespoon. I use no butter. And I use light margarine—not the fat-free variety—in crumble toppings and glazes.

If, however, you prefer a muffin made with more oil, feel free to add canola oil to sweet muffins or olive oil to savory muffins. For each tablespoon of added oil, the fat content increases by a little more than one gram per muffin. So, for example, if you add one-quarter cup (4 tablespoons) of canola oil to a recipe, each muffin will contain approximately four to five more grams of fat. Also, if you do add oil, be sure to reduce the other liquids by the same amount.

Finally, you may notice that I do not use fat-free margarines or spreads in my muffin recipes. I say this without reservation. I have made many attempts to create quality muffins using fat-free margarines in the batter, but the muffins were consistently rubbery and tough. I have also tried using these fat-free products to make crumble toppings and glazes. Without exception, the fat-free margarine turned crumble toppings into mush and glazes into watery soup. Fat-free margarines simply do not contain the properties necessary for successful muffin making.

TOOLS AND UTENSILS

Setting up the kitchen to bake muffins is like getting ready for a Sunday stroll in the park—you don't need much by way of supplies. Just a few simple tools and utensils, a minimal exertion of energy, and you are ready for a good time.

FOOD PROCESSOR

I have always been slow to embrace new fashions (maybe even a little hard-headed), but when I come around, I'm like a religious convert. When I was a freshman in college, for example, and the student government eliminated the dress code, I swore I'd never wear jeans to class. Three months later, mine were the most torn, patched, and jewel-studded jeans on campus.

I took to food processors in the same way. "Not me," I said, "I want to *feel* the food I'm chopping. It's strictly low-tech for me." Years later, I find I cannot live without my food processor. It's such a nifty little gadget. It blends, chops, grates, and pulverizes just about anything I feed it. If I feel weary or out of sorts, it smiles empathetically and says, "Let me do that for you, Sweety." I smile back gratefully and turn over the goods.

You will notice that most of my muffins are chock full of *goodies* (yummy little additions that make each muffin unique). My processor helps me prepare these goodies. It chops nuts and seeds, and grates vegetables, ginger root, and citrus peel. Sometimes I use my food processor to blend together a recipe's wet ingredients. If you think you will be baking a lot of muffins and you do not own a food processor, I strongly recommend that you get one. You will be very glad you did.

BOWLS AND SUCH

You need a few standard utensils—measuring cups, measuring spoons, and mixing bowls in assorted sizes. For muffins that call for veggies and fruit, you need a chopping surface and a sharp knife or two. A large wooden spoon is ideal for combining wet and dry ingredients and acts as an accurate measure for spooning the batter into the muffin cups.

If you do not have a food processor, use your favorite chopping and grating utensils to prepare veggies, fruits, and nuts. Utensils such as a potato ricer (for mashing) and a hand-operated grinder (for chopping and grinding nuts and/or spices) also will come in handy. You need a wire whisk to beat eggs and egg whites and to mix the other wet ingredients, and a hand-held grater to grate veggies.

Another important utensil for making successful muffins is a sifter. Despite what people say, whole-grain muffins can be relatively light and airy. One of the secrets is to sift the flour once or twice before combining it with the wet ingredients. Sifting also eliminates the clumps that are often found in baking powder, baking soda, and whole-grain flours.

Discover the value of sifting by conducting the following simple experiment. Take a cup of whole-wheat flour or whole-wheat pastry flour and sift it two times, measuring before and after each sifting. It grows, doesn't it? A cup of flour becomes 1⅛—even 1¼ cups! You see what sifting does? It fluffs the flour, kind of like whipping cream, and that fluffiness is passed on to the final product.

"But I don't like sifting," you whine.

I know. I know. But if you don't listen to me on this one, you will have to find out the hard way. And you will have to put up with the tentative accolades of friends and relations who haven't the heart to tell you that your whole-grain masterpieces weigh a ton. It's easier just to follow my suggestion. Get yourself a sifter. Okay?

MUFFIN TINS

Unless otherwise indicated, all of the recipes in this book yield a dozen muffins and require 3-inch muffin tins. It makes little difference if you use tin, iron, or nonstick pans. Baking time will be about the same. If, however, you use jumbo- or mini-muffin tins, you must adjust baking time accordingly. A standard recipe for a dozen muffins makes about three dozen mini-muffins and requires approximately 10 to 15 minutes baking time. The same recipe yields six jumbo muffins and requires about 20 to 25 minutes baking time. If you want to get fancy and use heart-shaped, shell-shaped, or other unusual-shaped tins, you will have to adjust the baking time accordingly. Read the manufacturer's suggestions and be willing to experiment a little. Your best bet is to watch your muffins closely as they bake.

BAKING CUPS

Here are the pros and cons on using baking cups: You can avoid the use of butter, margarine, or oil and cut down on cleanup time by using foil or paper baking cups. That's the good news. The bad news is that warm muffins tend to adhere to the baking cups. Often, after you peel away the paper, what's left is a crumbled core about the size of a donut hole. Very disappointing. You end up giving the muffin-coated paper to the dog and wondering if it was all worth the effort.

There is a way out. You can reduce the cling factor by cooling the muffins completely before you gobble them up.

"But," you say, "who wants to wait for them to cool?"

Admittedly, it is a dilemma. I tend not to use baking cups for this reason. If you use foil baking cups, please remember that you won't be able to reheat the muffins in a microwave oven (or feed the muffin-coated paper to the dog). This could be a factor if you plan to freeze your muffins for later use. (*See* Freezing and Reheating on page 27).

TIPS AND TECHNIQUES

When I sat down to write about the techniques of muffin-making, I thought I would have only a few tips to share. I mean muffins are so easy to make, how much is there to say? I soon realized, however, that lots of little details lie behind every successful batch. And it is these very tidbits of information that help make muffin-baking a breeze.

GET INGREDIENTS READY BEFOREHAND

Before you start, it's a good idea to double-check your supplies and make certain that you have everything you will need—especially the standard ingredients. One time I went to the grocery store three times just to bake two batches of muffins because I assumed I had the basics when I didn't.

Read the recipe to see if any of the ingredients call for special preparations. For example, one recipe might call for chopped roasted walnuts; another, grated orange peel. If you prepare these ingredients first and set them aside, the recipe will come together quickly and easily. Here are some tips:

■ **Preparing Citrus Peel and Ginger Root.** Orange peel, lemon peel, and ginger root can be grated in batches in your food processor and stored in the refrigerator for several weeks.

Peel an orange or lemon, remove most of the pith, and chop the rind into half-inch bits. Process the rind in a food processor using the purée blade until it resembles coarse meal. For ginger root, remove the tough outer skin and chop the ginger into one-inch pieces. Using the purée blade of a food processor, chop the ginger into fine pieces.

I bought some four-ounce plastic containers with lids that are perfect for storing citrus peel and ginger root. I use an orange-colored container for the orange peel, yellow for the lemon peel, and brown for the ginger root. Then when I am mixing up a batch of muffins that calls for one of these ingredients, I simply reach into the refrigerator and grab the right colored container.

■ **Preparing Nuts.** Whenever I buy nuts—walnuts, almonds, pecans, etc.— I roast them right away. First, I place the nuts in a single layer on an ungreased baking sheet. Then I pop them into a 275° F oven for about 20 minutes, stirring them occasionally so they don't burn. After cooling the nuts to room temperature, I coarsely chop them in my food processor, place them in one-quart canning jars, and store them in the back part of the refrigerator's bottom shelf—the dead zone, as I call it. What else can you put back there but things that you don't use every day? Again, I prepare the nuts so they are ready to grab whenever I need them.

■ **Preparing Banana Purée.** Does your grocery store sell ripe bananas at reduced prices? Mine, too. When this happens, I buy several pounds of these ripe fruits, take them home, and purée and freeze them for future use.

Here's a tip: purée and freeze the bananas in the quantities called for in your favorite muffin recipes. For example, both Better Banana (Nut) Bran Muffins and Bananas Foster Muffins call for three ripe bananas. Friends of the Earth Vegan Muffins calls for two ripe bananas. And the Tropical Fruit Muffins recipe calls for only one. I purée and freeze one to two bananas in recycled eight-ounce margarine tubs, and three bananas in recycled one-pint yogurt containers. Stored this way, puréed bananas will keep for up to three months. Then when I want to bake a banana muffin, all I have to do is defrost the container with the desired amount of purée. Be sure to label the containers stating the contents and the amount.

■ **Preparing Crystallized Ginger and Dried Fruits.** When it comes to crystallized ginger and dried fruit, you will have to use your judgment in determining how to chop them. Crystallized ginger can be chopped in the food processor but you must take care to do so lightly. If you process too hard or for too long, the ginger will become a paste. If the crystallized ginger is particularly fresh and/or soft, I don't recommend this method. Chop it by hand instead.

The same holds true for dried fruits. Gooey dried fruits like prunes, figs, and dates are better chopped by hand. If your dried apricots are moist, chop them by hand as well. The remaining dried fruits—apples, peaches, pears—

can be chopped in the food processor. Of course, pea-sized dried fruits such as raisins, cranberries, and raspberries don't need chopping.

■ **Preparing Crumble Toppings.** It seems that everybody loves muffins with crumble toppings, but nobody wants to take the time to prepare the crumble. I hope I've made it easy for you. Just follow the directions with each recipe.

Here's an added tip: Put the ingredients in a medium-sized bowl, slip a tape or CD into the player, sit yourself down on a barstool or chair in the kitchen and, with a pastry blender or two knives, cut the margarine into the dry ingredients until the crumble is the consistency you want. It takes only a song or two. Your choice of music, however, is extremely important in determining the success or failure of your crumble topping. Select music that makes you want to sing along. Personally, I find that Eric Clapton's *Unplugged*, Simon and Garfunkel's *Concert in the Park*, Van Morrison's *Moondance*, and anything by Peter, Paul, and Mary do the trick for me. You choose whatever turns you on.

SIFT THE DRY INGREDIENTS

Sifting is very important. My friend Nancy says she never got into the habit of sifting. I guess it's like flossing your teeth. If you don't develop the habit early in life, you may never do so. I asked her, "Don't you get clumps of baking soda or baking powder in your muffins that ruin the flavor?" She admitted that sometimes she does. The only way to avoid this is to SIFT, SIFT, SIFT. Sifting also fluffs the flour, making the final muffin product lighter. So do it.

ADD THE GOODIES AS INSTRUCTED

You will notice that some recipes require that you add the goodies to the dry ingredients, while other recipes have you add them to the wet ingredients. My general rule of thumb is as follows: Whenever the goodies include fresh fruits such as apples or blueberries, or sticky dried fruits such as prunes or figs, I add them to the dry ingredients and toss to coat them with flour. This does two things. It prevents these ingredients from bleeding into the rest of the muffin, creating an unattractive and often gooey effect. And it keeps these goodies from sinking to the bottom of the cup.

By contrast, whenever a recipe calls for small dried fruits such as raisins or cranberries, I add these goodies to the wet ingredients and stir to combine. This helps plump the dried fruit a little before baking and prevents the flour from collecting in the nooks and crannies, the wrinkles and crevices, of the dried goodies.

The exception is seen in those recipes that have both fresh and dried fruit in the goody list. For the sake of convenience, I add all of the goodies to the dry ingredients.

STIR THE DRY AND WET INGREDIENTS TOGETHER AS LITTLE AS POSSIBLE

When wheat flour is combined with a wet ingredient, then kneaded or stirred, a protein called gluten is formed. Gluten causes the mixture to become sticky and take on an elastic quality. This is why wheat flour is so suitable for making breads. By kneading the dough, we encourage the gluten to form, resulting in that spongy quality we like so much in bread.

But muffins are another matter. We don't want them to have that spongy texture, so we work to prevent the gluten from forming. We do this by stirring muffin batter as little as possible. This is why I emphasize preparing the wet ingredients and dry ingredients separately before combining them. Thus, the final mixing can be kept to minimum.

WHIP THE EGGS FIRST, IF YOU LIKE

As discussed under "Eggs and Egg Products," beginning on page 15, you can feel free to use one whole egg or two egg whites interchangeably in all my muffin recipes. All instructions have you blend the egg or egg whites with the other wet ingredients. However, you can pump up the volume (and the rising power) of an egg by whipping it before adding it to the batter. Here's how. Before blending the wet ingredients, whip the whole egg or egg whites in your food processor for about 15 seconds. The whole egg will become lighter in color and will increase slightly in volume. The egg whites will become milky and start to stiffen. After whipping the egg or egg whites, add the remaining wet ingredients to the food processor and pulse to blend. Then you can proceed with the recipe. Of you do not have a food processor, use a wire whisk to bring about similar results.

Again, this is an optional step. If you are in a hurry, it is not necessary to whip the egg or the egg whites separately. If you have the time, however, do it. I find that this method improves the texture of the finished product.

MAKE ONLY ONE BATCH OF MUFFINS AT A TIME

One may be tempted to double the ingredients of a muffin recipe to make more than one batch at a time. This is an especially attractive idea if you need to bake several dozen muffins and freeze some for later use.

While this may seem like a good idea, I don't think you will be happy with the results. Larger batches seem to require more mixing, which compromises the muffins' light texture.

I have a rule. Never mix more than one batch at a time. If you have a large oven and want to bake more than one batch at a time, fine. But mix the individual batches separately. Trust me. You will be happier with the results.

USE NONSTICK COOKING SPRAY ON MUFFIN TINS

I used to take a hard line on using nonstick cooking sprays to grease my muffin tins. I didn't use them because I didn't like the taste they left on my muffins. In addition, I felt they left a residue on the muffin tins that was difficult to remove. Well, I took some flack for my position from both friends and family alike. They have convinced me that nonstick cooking sprays have improved enough over the years to warrant their use in muffin making. They were right. Besides, cooking sprays sure are convenient to use!

Before filling the cups with batter, I spray the 10 cups around the perimeter of a 12-cup tin and fill these cups with batter first. Then, if there is still more batter, I spray and fill the remaining cups as needed. This saves your tin from turning black from baked-on grease. Of course, you can also spray all 12 cups and then wipe the unused ones with a paper towel before baking.

FILL THE MUFFIN TINS

I like a full, dome-shaped muffin. For this reason I fill my muffin cups nearly to the top with batter. Then, in the rising, they spread over the edge of the cup. If you prefer muffins that peak in the middle, fill the muffin tins two-thirds full. Each recipe will then produce more than the specified yield.

OVEN TEMPERATURE

Always be sure to preheat the oven at least 10 minutes before baking the muffins. The rising action must be quick and to the point, so preheating is essential. Center the muffin tin on a rack placed in the middle of the oven and—unless intructed otherwise—bake each batch for 15 to 20 minutes at 400° F. (Batter with large amounts of fruit tends to burn at this temperature and should be baked in a slightly cooler oven.) If your oven has a glass door, watching the muffins bake can be particularly exciting. I like to sit by the oven door and watch my muffins blossom. It's kind of like watching my amaryllis bloom!

If you don't pay proper attention to the oven temperature, your muffins will be topsy-turvy affairs. When the temperature is too low, the muffins will be flat in the middle. When it is too hot, the muffins will have uneven peaks that resemble chefs' hats that are leaning to one side (*see* Figure 1.1). If you are consistently having problems, check your oven's thermostat.

For best results when baking more than a dozen muffins at a time, bake each batch separately. If this is not possible and you need to bake more than one batch at a time, place the muffin tins side by side in the middle of the oven. If your oven is not wide enough to place the tins side by side, place one above the other, but switch and turn the tins when the muffins are half-baked.

Figure 1.1   Effect of Oven Temperature on Muffins

Correctly baked muffins will be straight-sided and slightly rounded on top (left). Flat muffins result when the oven temperature is too low (center). An oven that is too hot causes muffins to have uneven peaks (right).

ARE THEY DONE YET?

The muffins are done when they are fully cooked in the center, and you can usually tell just by looking at them. If you are not sure, press the center of one or two muffins. If they are not overly moist and they spring back after you apply pressure, they are fully cooked. You can also test by inserting a toothpick in the middle of one or two muffins and drawing it out. If the toothpick comes out clean (that is, if there is no wet or moist muffin batter clinging to it), your muffins are done.

COOL FOR 10 MINUTES

Be sure to wait 10 minutes before removing the muffins from their tins. The wait can be difficult—especially when you are hungry. However, if you remove the muffins too soon, they will lose their shape and may even collapse. Besides, hot muffins stick to the sides of the pans, and if you force them out before they are fully cooled, most likely you will break them apart in the process.

FREEZING AND REHEATING

If you want to freeze muffins for later use, simply wrap each cooled muffin securely in plastic wrap and place in a zip-lock bag. Four muffins fit nicely in a one-quart bag; nine fit in a gallon bag. I use half-inch labels to mark each muffin before freezing it. Once frozen, almost all muffins look alike! Wrapped this way, muffins will keep up to three months in the freezer.

Be sure to cool your muffins completely before wrapping and freezing them. Otherwise ice crystals will form inside the wrapper and your muffins will become gooey as they thaw.

To reheat frozen muffins, simply place them—wrapper and all—in a microwave oven on high for 30 to 50 seconds (time varies with each oven).

NUTRITION FACTS

It's no news that Americans need to pay more attention to their diets. Studies indicate that we consume far too many calories, too much fat, cholesterol, and sodium, and too little complex carbohydrates and fiber. We also eat too much of the wrong kind of protein to maintain a healthy diet. As a result, we are fatter and more prone to heart disease, high blood pressure, stroke, cancer, and diabetes than we have ever been. Studies also indicate that we do not get the recommended amount of calcium and iron necessary to maintain healthy bones and blood, or the potassium needed to regulate the heart. Success in establishing and maintaining a healthy diet requires that we adopt two standards. First, it is important to eat the proper foods in the proper proportions. The United States Department of Agriculture (USDA) offers a simple guide to daily food choices in the Food Guide Pyramid (*see* Figure 1.2. on the next page.) The pyramid prioritizes basic food categories, placing breads, cereals, and grains in the most important position at the base. When we bake and eat our own wholesome and nutritious muffins, we can be assured of meeting these nutrition requirements in a most enjoyable way.

Second, it is important to be knowledgeable about the nutritional makeup of the foods we eat. This includes knowing the recommended daily requirement for each nutrient and monitoring our intake. Each recipe in this book provides precise nutritional information for each muffin. This allows you, the health-conscious cook, to be sure of exactly what you are eating.

NUTRIENTS

Everyone's diet must contain four basic *nutrients*—water, complex carbohydrates, proteins, and fats—as well as *micronutrients*, which include vitamins and minerals. Nutrients and micronutrients fuel the body. A proper balance of these essentials is necessary for optimum health.

A Word About Calories

A calorie is an energy unit. Carbohydrates, protein, and fat provide the body with the energy it needs to function. This energy is measured in calories. There are 4 calories in every gram of protein, 4 calories in every gram of carbohydrate, and 9 calories in every gram of fat. On a gram-for-gram basis, fat is more than twice as fattening as carbohydrates or protein.

Because people's calorie needs depend on their weight, age, gender, activity level, and metabolic rate, these needs vary greatly from person to person. Most adults, though, must consume 13 to 15 calories per pound of body weight each day to maintain their weight. Of course, some people need even

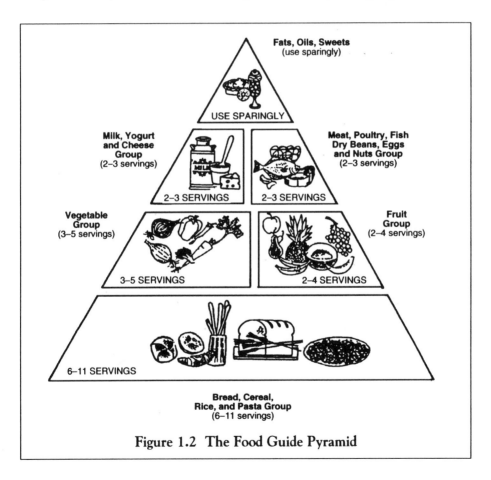

Figure 1.2 The Food Guide Pyramid

fewer calories, while very physically active people need more. (*See* Table 1.2 on page 32.)

I grew up during the years when low-calorie diets were popular. However, experts now say that low-calorie approaches to weight control without regard to other nutrient factors actually do more harm than good. For one thing, weight that is lost on a low-calorie diet is usually regained quickly. And many experts believe that low-calorie intake can make us more prone to health problems—less resistant to disease, more tired, and more likely to develop eating disorders. In order to maintain our weight we are encouraged to eat enough food to supply the appropriate amount of calories within our ideal caloric range. We are also advised to increase our activity level.

The muffins in this book range from 91 to 267 calories, with most containing 150 to 200. Generally, the heartier muffins are on the higher end of the calorie spectrum, while those that accompany other foods in a balanced meal (*see* Chapter 4, "Herby Cheesy Muffin Thangs") are on the lower end.

Fat

Fat is an essential nutrient. It is the most concentrated form of food energy we know. (As stated above, it provides 9 calories for every gram of fat as compared to only 4 calories per gram in protein or carbohydrates.) And, despite what many people think, we need fat in our diets. Fat provides fuel for the body, keeps us warm in cold weather, and helps with the assimilation and transport of important nutrients to our cells.

Why then is our consumption of fat such a concern these days? For one thing, most Americans eat far too much fat. Excess fat is a principal factor in weight gain because it is easily turned into body fat—more easily than excess protein or carbohydrates. And when fatty diets lead to obesity, diseases like diabetes and high blood pressure can result.

Specific types of fat present their own unique problems. For example, eating too much *saturated fat*—found in meat, butter, margarine, and other solid fats—raises blood cholesterol levels, setting the stage for heart disease. When eaten in excess, *polyunsaturated fats*—found mainly in vegetable oils like corn, sunflower, safflower, and soybean—can alter body chemistry to favor the development of blood clots, high blood pressure, and inflammatory diseases. Too much polyunsaturated fat can also promote free-radical damage to cells, contributing to heart disease and cancer. And *monounsaturated fats*—found mainly in vegetable and nut oils such as olive, peanut, and canola—have no known harmful effects other than being a concentrated source of calories, like all fats. In fact, they have been shown to reduce total blood cholesterol without lowering levels of the good cholesterol (high density lipoproteins or HDLs). Some monounsaturated fats have been shown to raise HDL levels.

Considering the problems caused by excess fat, one might think it would be best to eliminate it altogether. But the fact is that our bodies need some dietary fat. For instance, linoleic acid, a polyunsaturated fat naturally abundant in nuts and seeds, is essential for life. The average adult needs a minimum of 3 to 6 grams of linoleic acid per day (that's the amount found in one to two teaspoons of polyunsaturated vegetable oil or one to two tablespoons of nuts or seeds). Linolenic acid, a fat present mainly in fish and green plants, is also essential for good health. Some dietary fat is also necessary to help us absorb fat-soluble nutrients like vitamin E.

The USDA recommends limiting our fat intake to no more than 30 percent of our daily caloric level. Some experts believe that 20 to 25 percent is even better in most cases. So the amount of fat you should eat every day is based on the number of calories you need. As previously mentioned in the discussion on calories, although calorie needs vary from person to person, most adults consume 13 to 15 calories per pound each day to maintain their weight.

Once you have determined your calorie requirements, you can establish a fat budget for yourself. Suppose you are a moderately active adult who weighs 150 pounds. You will probably need around 15 calories per pound to maintain your weight, or about 2,250 calories per day (150 pounds x 15 calories = 2,250 calories). To limit your fat intake to no more than 20 percent of your total daily calories, you can eat no more than 450 calories derived from fat per day (2,250 total calories x .20 percent fat = 450 fat calories). To convert this calorie count to grams of fat, divide by 9, as one fat gram has 9 calories. Therefore, you should limit yourself to 50 grams of fat per day (450 fat calories ÷ 9 calories per gram = 50 grams).

Table 1.2 on page 32 shows two maximum daily fat-gram budgets—one based on 20 percent of calorie intake and one based on 25 percent. If you are overweight, go by the weight you would like to be. This will allow you to eventually reach your goal weight.

In my first book, *Gloria's Glorious Muffins*, I focused on keeping the saturated fat content of my muffins low by limiting the use of ingredients such as margarine and butter. In this book, I have taken things a step further by

Table 1.2 Maximum Daily Fat Intakes*

Weight (pounds)	Daily Calorie Intake (13–15 calories per pound)	Fat Grams Allowed (20% of Calorie Intake)	Fat Grams Allowed (25% of Calorie Intake)
100	1,300–1,500	29–33	36–42
110	1,430–1,650	32–37	40–46
120	1,560–1,800	34–40	43–50
130	1,690–1,950	38–43	47–54
140	1,820–2,100	40–46	51–58
150	1,950–2,250	43–50	54–62
160	2,080–2,400	46–53	58–67
170	2,.210-2,550	49–57	61–71
180	2,340–2,700	52–60	65–75
190	2,470–2,850	55–63	69–79
200	2,600–3,000	58–66	72–83

* Maximum Daily Fat Intakes chart, as well as much of the information on fats and calories has been reprinted from *Secrets of Fat-Free Cooking* by Sandra Woodruff, R.D. (Garden City Park, NY: Avery Publishing Group, 1995.)

dramatically reducing all fat. Nearly all of the muffins in this book contain 3 grams of fat or less. (The few exceptions include muffins that contain an optional nut ingredient.) While it is true that nuts have a high-fat content, they are also a fabulous source of dietary fiber and essential linoleic acid. (*See* Crazy About Nuts and Seeds, beginning on page 82.) You might also be interested to know that even the muffins with small amounts of saturated fat, such as those with crumb toppings or glazes, contain less than 3 grams of fat! And, with few exceptions, my muffins derive less than 15 percent (with more than half deriving less than 10 percent) of their total calories from fat.

Cholesterol

Cholesterol is a white, waxy, fatty substance found in all foods that come from animal sources. Our bodies need cholesterol, which helps to build cell membranes, to produce hormones, and to manufacture bile acids. The liver is capable of manufacturing all of the cholesterol needed for good health. Too much cholesterol in our diets tends to clog the arteries and obstruct the flow of blood from the heart, putting us at risk for high blood pressure, stroke, and heart disease.

Studies indicate that lowering cholesterol intake may help to reduce these risks. The FDA and the USDA recommend that we consume no more than 300 milligrams of cholesterol daily. This corresponds with the recommendations of the American Heart Association, the National Academy of Sciences, and the National Institutes of Health.*

I found that I could keep the cholesterol in my muffins low—from 0 to 20 milligrams per muffin—by using only two egg whites or one whole egg in each recipe. (It is the yolk that contains the cholesterol. Muffins that include the whole egg contain up to 20 milligrams of cholesterol each. Those made with egg whites only contain very little or no cholesterol.) There are only seven muffins in this book that contain between 20 and 25 milligrams of cholesterol. These recipes include ingredients such as cheese or oil.

I am very pleased with these results. According to federal regulations, any food that contains 20 milligrams or less of cholesterol and 2 grams or less of saturated fat per serving is considered a low-cholesterol food. (*See* Guide to Nutrient Claims on page 34.) This means that you can enjoy my muffins every day without feeling one ounce of guilt.

Protein

Proteins, derived from the Greek word meaning "primary," and the amino acids from which they are formed are often called the building blocks of life—so important is the role they play in building and repairing tissues and cells. They are also involved in transporting nutrients throughout the body, clotting blood, and manufacturing antibodies. Proteins are found in every system of the body. In fact, with the exception of water and sometimes fat, protein is the body's most plentiful substance.

* These organizations recommend that people with severe high blood cholesterol or heart disease limit their cholesterol intake even further.

We derive protein from foods that are also sources of fat, cholesterol, and carbohydrates. What concerns nutrition experts is that since the early part of the century, Americans have shifted their primary source of protein from grains and flours (foods high in carbohydrates) to meats and cheeses (foods high in fat and cholesterol). Experts point to this shift in the dietary sources of protein as the principal cause of increased diet-related diseases.

Our task, as nutrition-conscious individuals, is to get our recommended protein from foods that are good sources of carbohydrates but do not exceed

Guide to Nutrient Claims

Under current FDA and USDA regulations, the nutrient content of fat, cholesterol, and fiber is defined as follows:

FAT

- **Fat free.** The product has less than 0.5 gram of fat per serving.
- **Low-fat.** The product has no more than 3 grams of fat per serving.

CHOLESTEROL

- **Cholesterol-free.** The product has less than 2 milligrams of cholesterol and no more than 2 grams of saturated fat per serving
- **Low-cholesterol.** The product has no more than 20 milligrams of cholesterol and 2 grams of saturated fat per serving.

FIBER

- **High in fiber.** The product has 5 grams or more of fiber per serving (at least 20 percent of the recommended daily amount).
- **Good source of fiber.** The product has 2.5 to 4.9 grams of fiber per serving (10 to 19 percent of the recommended daily amount).

the maximum requirements of fat and cholesterol. This is accomplished by getting protein from vegetable sources such as grains and cereals and consuming only low-fat animal products such as skim or low-fat milk, nonfat yogurt, and reduced-fat cheese.

Exactly how much protein should we eat? Only about 10 to 15 percent of our daily calories should come from protein. In other words, based on 2,000- and 2,500-calorie diets, 200 to 375 of our daily calories should come from protein.

The recommended dietary allowance for protein is not a set figure applicable to all people. That is, it is calculated individually according to our ideal body weight, and it diminishes as we grow older. To calculate the daily recommendation for protein, we must multiply our ideal body weight by a recommended allowance of protein per pound of that weight. The figures, established by the Food and Nutrition Board of the National Academy of Sciences, are as follows: ages 19 and over, 0.36 gram of protein per pound of ideal body weight; ages 15–18, 0.39 gram; ages 11–14, 0.45 gram; ages 7–10, 0.55 gram; ages 4–6, 0.68 gram; ages 1–3, 0.81 gram; ages 6 months–1 year, 0.90 gram; ages 0–6 months, 1.00 gram. The only exception is for pregnant and nursing women, who have special protein needs. For them, calculations should be based on 0.62 gram and 0.53 gram of protein respectively per pound of ideal body weight.

Calculated accordingly, the recommended allowance of proteins for adults varies significantly from, for example, 39.6 grams daily for the 110-pound adult (110 pounds x 0.36 grams per pound) to 72 grams daily for the 200-pound adult (200 pounds x 0.36 grams per pound).

Given these protein facts, I know you will agree that it is important to get the right amount of protein from the right sources. Gloria's Gourmet Low-Fat Muffins fit the protein bill. Most of the muffins contain 5 to 7 grams of protein, derived primarily from vegetable sources. You can feel confident in the fact that you are eating a balanced food product.

Carbohydrates

Carbohydrates are starches and sugars that provide much of the vitamins, minerals, and fiber we need each day. They are found in such foods as breads, cereals, flours, pasta, rice, barley, and vegetables. Natural carbohydrates are usually divided into two categories: complex carbohydrates and natural sugars.

Complex carbohydrates, which provide the body with the energy it needs to function, are found primarily in beans and grains. They supply many of the nutrients our bodies need. Natural sugars are carbohydrates found in fresh fruits and vegetables. These are also high in nutrients and supply much-needed energy for the body.

You may find it interesting that while excess calories, fat, cholesterol, and even protein have been directly or indirectly linked with one major disease or another, no disease has been linked with eating too many carbohydrates. Our bodies thrive on wholesome carbohydrates and there is every indication that we should consume a great deal of them.

But what has concerned experts in the past several decades has been a dramatic shift in emphasis from foods that contain natural, high-nutrient carbohydrates to nutrient-deficient, high-calorie foods made primarily of refined or processed carbohydrates. Like the unhappy consequences of our shift from plant protein to animal protein, this shift from natural carbohydrates to those found in processed foods has been linked unfavorably with many of our growing health problems.

According to the USDA, complex carbohydrates should constitute from 55 to 60 percent of our daily diet. This means that 1,100 to 1,500 of our daily calories (based on 2,000- and 2,500-calorie diets) should come from natural carbohydrates.

The muffins in this book are made with wholesome and natural ingredients, contain little or no processed or refined products, and supply the energy and nutrients our bodies need from sources that are close to nature. Enjoying whole-grain muffins is a delicious way to increase your daily intake of useful carbohydrates.

Fiber

Dietary fiber is a complex carbohydrate. It is found in plants—in the outer layers of cereal grains, and the fibrous parts of fruits, beans, and other vegetables. Referred to in the past as *roughage*, fiber is actually the part of the plant materials that our body cannot digest. Yet, fiber is known to perform a number of important functions. It promotes feelings of fullness; prevents constipation, hemorrhoids, and other intestinal problems; and is associated with a reduced incidence of colon cancer. In addition, fiber may help lower blood cholesterol levels, reducing the risk of heart disease.

The recommended amount of daily fiber is approximately 25 grams. This is based on FDA and USDA reference amounts of 11.5 grams of fiber per 1,000 calories. But most American adults eat only 4 to 6 grams of fiber each day. Experts agree that we need to do better.

According to standards established by the FDA, a high-fiber food is one that contains 5 grams or more of fiber per serving. Foods that contain 2.5 to 4.9 grams per serving are considered good fiber sources. I paid close attention to these standards while creating the muffins for this book. It was fascinating to see how different flours altered the muffins' fiber content. Whole-wheat flour contains four times as much fiber per measure as unbleached white flour and 30 percent more than whole-wheat pastry flour. If, when creating a new muffin, I realized that the fiber content of a recipe was not as high as I wanted it to be, I adjusted the whole-wheat flour to bring the final products up to snuff. As a result, nearly all of my muffins are good sources of fiber. Many are considered high in fiber.

Sodium

Sodium, a mineral contained in many foods, plays a key role in maintaining proper fluid levels in the body. It is also involved in the transmission of nerve impulses and has been shown to be a major factor in controlling high blood pressure.

The FDA's recommended daily limit for sodium is 2,400 milligrams, while the American Heart Association recommends no more than 3,000 milligrams for healthy adults. To give you an idea of how much sodium that is, consider that one teaspoon of table salt contains approximately 2,000 milligrams of sodium! Most American adults, however, eat much more—between 3,000 and 7,000 milligrams per day. Experts agree that most people would benefit greatly from reducing the sodium in their diets.

Fortunately, it is easier than ever to keep track of our sodium intake. New food labels clearly list the sodium content of all food items. And by preparing our own foods instead of buying commercially prepared foods, which are usually high in sodium, we can control our sodium intake even further. Only about one-third of the sodium we consume comes from the food itself, while the remaining two-thirds is added either during cooking or at the table.

A reasonable amount of sodium is 240 milligrams to 450 milligrams per serving. The sodium content in *Gloria's Gourmet Low-Fat Muffins* is at the low end of (and even below) this range.

Potassium

Potassium, an important mineral contained in many foods, is needed for the healthy, steady functioning of the nervous system. Potassium helps to regulate proper muscle control—especially for our most important muscle, the heart. It also helps to assimilate the energy derived from the foods we eat. Potassium plays an important role in transmitting nerve impulses, and studies indicate that it may be significant in reducing high blood pressure.

The recommended daily value for potassium is 3,500 milligrams. Foods high in potassium contain about 350 milligrams to 665 milligrams per serving. By these standards, most of the muffins in this book are good sources of potassium. If you want to select muffins with high-potassium content, choose those made with dried fruits, bananas, yogurt, and/or nuts.

Iron

Because of the key role it plays in oxygen transfer in the blood, iron is considered the most important mineral in our bodies. When we are deficient in iron, our organs and tissues do not have the proper supply of oxygen, and, therefore, lack the energy needed to function. Children and women (particularly pregnant women) need more iron than others.

The recommended daily intake for iron is 18 milligrams. In order to maintain a constant, daily supply of iron, it is important to eat foods that are good iron sources. The iron content in my gourmet muffins ranges from about 1.0 milligram to 3.0 milligrams. Those muffins with high-iron content are the ones containing figs, sweet potatoes, and/or prunes.

Calcium

Calcium is critical in the formation of strong bones and teeth. Recent studies indicate that high calcium intake may also help decrease the risk of heart attack, colon cancer, and stroke, and that it may play a significant role in lowering high blood pressure and maintaining healthy skin.

Calcium is considered an especially critical dietary nutrient for women. It is now believed that a low intake of calcium by young women contributes to the low bone mass associated with osteoporosis in later life.

The recommended daily allowance for calcium is 800 to 1,000 milligrams for all adults ages twenty-five to sixty-five. Postmenopausal women who are not on hormone replacement therapy and all adults over sixty-five should consume 1,500 milligrams of calcium daily. However, recent studies indicate that most American woman consume far less—only 500 to 600 milligrams per day.

Foods that contain 90 to 190 milligrams of calcium per serving are considered good calcium sources. All of the muffins in this book contain between 50 and 150 milligrams of calcium.

READY, SET, GO!

Now that you are armed with important muffin-making guidelines and other useful information, you are ready to begin. Have fun and enjoy!

2.

FRESH & FRUITY, SOMETIMES NUTTY, ANYTIME MUFFINS

I had a hard time waking up this morning. A thick fog clouded my mind as I stumbled to the bathroom. When I looked in the mirror through dilated eyes, the face looking back could barely see me. "I need coffee," I said to myself. I groped my way to the kitchen, grabbed a bag of coffee beans that my friend Douglas had given me, filled the grinder, put the lid in place, and pressed the lever. Nothing happened.

"Hmm." I could scarcely think my way through this one. I checked the electrical connection. It seemed to be okay. I pushed the lever again. Still nothing. I decided to try depressing the switch with a shish-kabob skewer to see if I could start the machine that way. I should mention that I neglected to remove the beans from the grinder before doing so.

The blades whirred and the centrifugal force sent coffee beans flying through the kitchen. There were beans in the opened drawers, in the sink, on the window sill, in my eyes, and on the floor four feet away. Later, I even found some in my pockets. The machine itself was empty.

"This isn't working," I thought. "I need to wake up before I tackle such complex life functions." I sat on the couch with the basket of muffins I had baked the night before—Blueberries, Oats, and Cream. I unwrapped one, bit into it, and BOING. It was like pressing the "open" switch of an automatic garage-door opener. The flavors of blueberries, oats, and cream consumed my attention and suddenly the fog that had clouded my awareness lifted. "Ah, yes," I thought. "I remember this. This is morning."

I had morning in mind when I created my "Fresh & Fruity, Sometimes Nutty, Anytime Muffins." Their rich flavors and textures will get your attention every time and help you start your day with a little vitality and awareness—not to mention a smile. But don't limit yourself to breakfast. You can enjoy these flavorful creations any time of night or day.

Apple Ginger Muffins

I began using crystallized ginger in so many of my new muffins, at one point, I worried I might be getting a little carried away. I can get like that. I discover something I really like and then I latch on to it—like the Alien embryo latched onto John Hurt's face. I try to squeeze every ounce of life out of the things I enjoy and sometimes I get fanatical. But after a thorough examination of my conscience, I decided my fondness for crystallized ginger isn't really a problem. I mean, I'm not obsessed; I just really like it. I've liked crystallized ginger from the first time I bit into it and felt it burn inside my mouth. Like a sip of good cognac, it tingles all the way down to the stomach. And what a fabulous muffin it makes! See for yourself what I mean.

Dry Ingredients	Wet Ingredients
1 cup whole-wheat pastry flour	1 cup skim milk
¾ cup whole-wheat flour	½ cup applesauce
¾ cup unbleached white flour	½ cup honey
1 teaspoon baking powder	1 large egg
1 teaspoon baking soda	1 teaspoon vanilla extract
1 teaspoon ground ginger	1 teaspoon grated lemon peel
¼ teaspoon sea salt	

Goodies

1 medium apple, peeled and chopped (do not grate)
3 tablespoons coarsely chopped crystallized ginger

Yield: 11–12 muffins

1. Preheat the oven to 400° F.

2. Sift the dry ingredients together in a large bowl. Add the goodies and toss to coat.

3. Whisk the wet ingredients in a medium bowl or blend them in a food processor. Pour the wet ingredients into the dry mixture. Stir just until mixed. *Do not overstir.*

4. Spoon the batter into a greased or papered muffin tin. Fill each cup nearly to the top.

5. Bake for 15 to 20 minutes.

6. Cool the muffins at least 10 minutes before removing from the tin.

NUTRITIONAL FACTS (per 93-gram muffin)
Calories: 168 (5% from fat)

Fat: 1 g	Cholesterol: 20 mg	Carbohydrates: 38 g
Protein: 4 g	Fiber: 2.6 g	Sodium: 240 mg
Potassium: 218 mg	Iron: 1.2 mg	Calcium: 73 mg

Berry Berry Delicious Muffins

At the end of last summer, my friend Barbara informed me that Eckerd's, one of the drugstore chains in our area, was having a sale on Celestial Seasonings Iced Delight teas. We all know that their teas are fabulous, but at three or four dollars a box I can't always afford to treat myself. This time, however, because of a special summer clearance, the Iced Delight was only 99¢ a box. Strike while the iron is hot. Right? I hurried over to Eckerd's and bought a few boxes each of Caribbean Oasis and Cranberry Razz. After sampling a chilled glass of each, I dashed back to buy up the entire stock—twelve boxes of Caribbean Oasis and ten of Cranberry Razz!

Now, I'd like to say that I selflessly shared my stash with others. However, except for an occasional gift to family and friends, I kept all the tea for myself. I can't remember enjoying a summer beverage so much. And my Berry Berry Delicious Muffins were inspired by Cranberry Razz Iced Delight.

Dry Ingredients	Wet Ingredients
¾ cup whole-wheat pastry flour	1 cup skim milk
¾ cup whole-wheat flour	½ cup apple juice
¾ cup unbleached white flour	½ cup nonfat sour cream
¼ cup light brown sugar	¼ cup honey
1½ teaspoons baking soda	2 large egg whites
1 teaspoon baking powder	2 teaspoons grated lemon peel
½ teaspoon nutmeg	1 teaspoon vanilla extract
¼ teaspoon sea salt	
¼ cup oat or wheat bran	

Goodies

½ cup dried raspberries
½ cup dried cranberries

Yield: 12 muffins

1. Preheat the oven to 400° F.

2. Sift all of the dry ingredients, except the oat or wheat bran, together in a large bowl. Add the bran and stir to combine.

3. Whisk the wet ingredients in a medium bowl or blend them in a food processor. Add the goodies and stir to combine.

4. Pour the wet mixture into the dry ingredients. Stir just until mixed. *Do not overstir.*

5. Spoon the batter into a greased or papered muffin tin. Fill each cup nearly to the top.

6. Bake for 15 to 20 minutes.

7. Cool the muffins at least 10 minutes before removing from the tin.

NUTRITIONAL FACTS (per 94-gram muffin)
Calories: 142 (3% from fat)

Fat: <1 g	Cholesterol: <1 mg	Carbohydrates: 32 g
Protein: 5 g	Fiber: 3.0 g	Sodium: 256 mg
Potassium: 222 mg	Iron: 1.2 mg	Calcium: 78 mg

Better Banana (Nut) Bran Muffins

This recipe calls for ripe bananas. How can you tell if bananas are ripe enough? Look for those with lots of brown specks on their outer skin but not so many specks that they merge together to make the banana completely brown. Remove the skin, chop the banana into about four or five big chunks, put the chunks into your food processor, and then blend.

When you bake these muffins, let the batter sit about 10 minutes before you pop them into the oven. I have found that the bran needs a little time to absorb the banana goodness before baking. If you allow this extra time, you will bake a moist, delectable muffin every time.

You may notice that the walnuts in this recipe are optional. Without the nuts, each muffin contains less than 1 gram of fat, ranking them among the lowest in fat in this book. With the nuts, they are still low in fat, with 4 grams per muffin. For more information about using nuts in muffins, see Crazy About Nuts and Seeds beginning on page 82.

Dry Ingredients	Wet Ingredients
1 cup unbleached white flour	3 ripe bananas, mashed
½ cup whole-wheat flour	(or 1½ cups)
¾ cup light brown sugar	¾ cup water
1 teaspoon baking powder	2 large egg whites
1 teaspoon baking soda	1½ teaspoons vanilla extract
¼ teaspoon sea salt	1 teaspoon grated lemon peel,
1 cup wheat bran	or ½ teaspoon lemon extract

Goodies

½ cup chopped roasted walnuts (optional)

Yield: 11–12 muffins

1. Preheat the oven to 400° F.

2. Sift all of the dry ingredients, except the wheat bran, together in a large bowl. Add the bran and walnuts (if using) and stir to combine.

3. Whisk the wet ingredients in a medium bowl or blend them in a food processor.Pour the wet ingredients into the dry mixture. Stir just until mixed. *Do not overstir.*

4. Spoon the batter into a greased or papered muffin tin. Fill each cup nearly to the top.

5. Bake for 15 to 20 minutes.

6. Cool the muffins at least 10 minutes before removing from the tin.

NUTRITIONAL FACTS (per 93-gram muffin without walnuts)
Calories: 153 (2% from fat)

Fat: <1 g	Cholesterol: 0 mg	Carbohydrates: 34 g
Protein: 4 g	Fiber: 3.7 g	Sodium: 205 mg
Potassium: 324 mg	Iron: 1.6 mg	Calcium: 48 mg

NUTRITIONAL FACTS (per 98-gram muffin with walnuts)
Calories: 188 (18% from fat)

Fat: 4 g	Cholesterol: 0 mg	Carbohydrates: 38 g
Protein: 5 g	Fiber: 4.3 g	Sodium: 205 mg
Potassium: 352 mg	Iron: 1.7 mg	Calcium: 53 mg

Black Cherry Blossom Muffins

There's no way around it. . . pitting cherries is a drag. Even if you do as my friend Nancy does and use a mechanical pitter, removing the stones from cherries takes some effort. I think, however, that once you've tried my Black Cherry Blossom Muffins you will agree that the effort is well worth it.

For these out-of-sight muffins, choose firm, fresh cherries that are in season. When preparing cherries, you may want to wear rubber gloves, as the dark juice will stain your hands. Begin by cutting each cherry in half and removing the pit. Then cut each half lengthwise. Finally, cut across the middle of each lengthwise slice. You will have eight currant-sized pieces from each cherry.

If you want to make these muffins when cherries are not in season, use pitted canned or frozen varieties. The only difference is that these cherries will bleed into the muffins a bit. If using canned cherries, be sure to drain them well before measuring and chopping. If using frozen, defrost and drain them before using.

Dry Ingredients	Wet Ingredients
1½ cups unbleached white flour	¾ cup skim milk
1 cup whole-wheat flour	½ cup applesauce
2 teaspoons baking soda	½ cup honey
½ teaspoon baking powder	2 large egg whites
¼ teaspoon sea salt	2 teaspoons cherry flavoring
⅛ teaspoon ground mace	2 teaspoons grated lemon peel
¼ cup oat or wheat bran	1 teaspoon vanilla extract

Goodies

1 cup dark sweet cherries, pitted and chopped

Yield: 11–12 muffins

1. Preheat the oven to 375° F.

2. Sift all of the dry ingredients, except the oat or wheat bran, together in a large bowl. Add the bran and stir to combine. Add the goodies and toss to coat.

3. Whisk the wet ingredients in a medium bowl or blend them in a food processor. Pour the wet ingredients into the dry mixture. Stir just until mixed. *Do not overstir.*

4. Spoon the batter into a greased or papered muffin tin. Fill each cup nearly to the top.

5. Bake for 15 to 20 minutes.

6. Cool the muffins at least 10 minutes before removing from the tin.

NUTRITIONAL FACTS (per 91-gram muffin)
Calories: 164 (3% from fat)

Fat: 1 g	Cholesterol: <1 mg	Carbohydrates: 37 g
Protein: 5 g	Fiber: 2.9 g	Sodium: 301 mg
Potassium: 197 mg	Iron: 1.3 mg	Calcium: 44 mg

Blueberries, Oats, and Cream Muffins

When blueberries are in season, one of my favorite breakfasts is a nice warm bowl of oatmeal with fresh blueberries and a dollop of sour cream. I used to feel a little guilty about the sour cream—like I do when I smear real butter and sour cream on my baked potato. But now that we can buy sour cream in the nonfat variety, there need be no guilt involved.

Nonfat sour cream is one of the few nonfat dairy items that, in my opinion, is nearly as good as the fattier version—at least for baking. And nonfat sour cream does wonderful things in muffins. It seems to make the muffins lighter while its richness comes through in every bite.

I've made these muffins with both rolled oats and oat bran to ensure that the nutty oat flavor comes through. Because oats contain a natural antioxidant, these muffins stay fresh longer than muffins without oats.

Dry Ingredients	Wet Ingredients
1¼ cups whole-wheat flour	1 cup nonfat sour cream
½ cup unbleached white flour	1 cup water
½ cup light brown sugar	1 large egg
1½ teaspoons baking soda	½ cup honey
1 teaspoon baking powder	2 teaspoons grated lemon peel
½ teaspoon ground cinnamon	1 teaspoon vanilla extract
¼ teaspoon sea salt	
¾ cup rolled oats	
¼ cup oat bran	

Goodies
¾ cup firm fresh blueberries, washed and patted dry

Yield: 12 muffins

1. Preheat the oven to 400° F.

2. Sift all of the dry ingredients, except the rolled oats and oat bran, together in a large bowl. Add the oats and bran and stir to combine. Add the blueberries and toss to coat.

3. Whisk the wet ingredients in a medium bowl or blend them in a food processor. Pour the wet ingredients into the dry mixture. Stir just until mixed. *Do not overstir.*

4. Spoon the batter into a greased or papered muffin tin. Fill each cup nearly to the top.

5. Bake for 15 to 20 minutes.

6. Cool the muffins at least 10 minutes before removing from the tin.

NUTRITIONAL FACTS (per 103-gram muffin)
Calories: 192 (6% from fat)

Fat: 1 g	Cholesterol: 18 mg	Carbohydrates: 43 g
Protein: 5 g	Fiber: 2.9 g	Sodium: 258 mg
Potassium: 216 mg	Iron: 1.4 mg	Calcium: 70 mg

Buckwheat Buttermilk Muffins with Blueberries and Maple Syrup

You never know when the creativity bug is going to bite. There I was minding my own business, sitting in front of the mirror at the beauty school where I get my hair cut. Tanya, my hairdresser, was totally absorbed in the finer details of my new no-nonsense summer "do." Casually I asked her if she had anything special planned for the Labor Day weekend.

"You bet," she replied, still intent on her work and looking somewhat like a mad scientist, her head flung back as she peered through granny glasses that were perched precariously on the tip of her nose. "Me and Ingram are probably going to go mess around on the Blue Ridge Parkway. We're going to get an early start so we can make it to Mabry Mill for a breakfast of buckwheat pancakes with fresh blueberries and maple syrup."

What can I say? That's how muffins are born.

Dry Ingredients	Wet Ingredients
1 cup whole-wheat flour	1 cup nonfat buttermilk
¾ cup unbleached white flour	1 cup maple syrup
¾ cup buckwheat flour	2 large egg whites
1½ teaspoons baking soda	1 teaspoon grated orange peel
1 teaspoon baking powder	
¼ teaspoon sea salt	

Goodies

¾ cup firm fresh blueberries, washed and patted dry

Yield: 11–12 muffins

1. Preheat the oven to 400° F.

2. Sift the dry ingredients in a large bowl. Add the blueberries and toss to coat.

3. Whisk the wet ingredients in a medium bowl or blend them in a food processor. Pour the wet ingredients into the dry mixture. Stir just until mixed. *Do not overstir.*

4. Spoon the batter into a greased or papered muffin tin. Fill each cup nearly to the top.

5. Bake for 15 to 20 minutes.

6. Cool the muffins at least 10 minutes before removing from the tin.

NUTRITIONAL FACTS (per 91-gram muffin)
Calories: 185 (3% from fat)

Fat: 1 g	Cholesterol: 0 mg	Carbohydrates: 42 g
Protein: 5 g	Fiber: 2.7 g	Sodium: 280 mg
Potassium: 213 mg	Iron: 1.4 mg.	Calcium: 82 mg

A Bit About Buttermilk

You may notice that many of my recipes call for buttermilk. That's because it is truly a miracle ingredient. A tad acidic, buttermilk gives the rising agents a boost. You can often observe your muffins beginning to rise even before you put them in the oven. And buttermilk lends its thick, creamy texture to whatever it meets; it gives muffins a light, biscuit-like quality. Despite the fact that it has little or no fat (you can buy both low-fat and nonfat varieties) and comparatively little cholesterol (*see* Table 2.1, Nutrient Analysis of Milk Varieties, on page 55), adding buttermilk to muffins reduces the need for fats and oils. It is also low in calories and loaded with calcium and protein. See what I mean about being a miracle ingredient?

In the good old days when people churned their own butter, buttermilk was truly buttermilk. That is, it was the by-product of the butter-making process. Traditionally, one would churn sour milk until the fatty component, butter, solidified. What remained was a liquid residue that often contained some flecks of butter. Depending on how well it was strained, the buttermilk would be either very low in fat or completely fat-free. Because it was made from sour milk, which made it easier for the butter to solidify, the buttermilk had a tangy or outright sour taste.

Today if you wanted authentic buttermilk, you would probably have to make your own butter—or make friends with someone who does! Virtually all the buttermilk sold today is produced by adding bacteria cultures to low-fat or skim milk. The process, much like the yogurt-making process, produces lactic acid and acidophilus bacteria. This makes buttermilk more easily digested by people who are lactose intolerant.

Table 2.1   Nutrient Analysis of Milk Varieties

The nutritional breakdown of the following milk varieties is based on 8-ounce (1 cup) servings.

Milk Type	Calories	Fat gms	Chol. mgs	Protein gms	Calcium mgs
Nonfat Buttermilk	90	0	5	9	250
Low-Fat Buttermilk	99	2	9	9	285
Skim Milk	86	<1	4	8	302
1% Low-Fat Milk	102	3	10	8	300
2% Low-Fat Milk	121	5	18	8	297
Whole Milk	150	8	33	8	291

Catherine's Lemon Red Raspberry Muffins

Niece Catherine, as I like to call her when she calls me Aunt Gloria, turned me on to the delicate French hard candies called pastilles. They are the pea-sized fruit-shaped candy drops that come in round tins that fit neatly in the palm of your hand. Very chic. The way Catherine twisted the lid and presented the tin of treats before me reminded me of the way movie stars offered each other cigarettes in 1940's films. "Pastille?" "Oh, thank you, darling. Don't mind if I do."

Catherine got into the pastille habit during the years she was learning to play the piano. She and my sister Betty always had season tickets to the children's concert series at Lincoln Center for the Performing Arts. As these candies had no crinkly wrappers that might disturb the people around them, they were the only ones my sister let Catherine take to the concerts. The candies come in all sorts of fruit flavors—orange, peach, cherry, grape. But Catherine's favorites are lemon and raspberry.

Catherine's Lemon Red Raspberry Muffins are for Niece Catherine. Thanks for the times when we painted our toenails and put blue mud on our faces and did all those primpy things that girls do to be close to each other. I don't care what they say about you, I think you're great! (Ha! Ha! Gotcha.)

By the way, these muffins look especially attractive with a light sprinkling of powdered sugar. Be sure to cool the muffins completely before adding the sugar.

Dry Ingredients	Wet Ingredients
1 cup whole-wheat pastry flour	1 cup nonfat buttermilk
1 cup unbleached white flour	½ cup applesauce
½ cup whole-wheat flour	½ cup honey
½ cup sugar	1 large egg
1½ teaspoons baking powder	2½ tablespoons
1 teaspoon baking soda	grated lemon peel
¼ teaspoon sea salt	

Goodies

¾ cup firm fresh raspberries* (about 6 ounces), washed, patted dry, and halved

* Can use frozen raspberries that have been thawed, drained, and patted dry.

Yield: 11–12 muffins

1. Preheat the oven to 375° F.

2. Sift the dry ingredients together in a large bowl. Add the raspberries and toss to coat.

3. Whisk the wet ingredients in a medium bowl or blend them in a food processor. Pour the wet ingredients into the dry mixture. Stir just until mixed, taking care not to break the raspberries or cause their juice to color the batter. *Do not overstir.*

4. Spoon the batter into a greased or papered muffin tin. Fill each cup nearly to the top.

5. Bake for 15 to 20 minutes.

6. Cool the muffins at least 10 minutes before removing from the tin.

NUTRITIONAL FACTS (per 88-gram muffin)
Calories: 185 (4% from fat)

Fat: 1 g	Cholesterol: 19 mg	Carbohydrates: 43 g
Protein: 4 g	Fiber: 2.7 g	Sodium: 226 mg
Potassium: 137 mg	Iron: 1.2 mg	Calcium: 81 mg

Cherry Irish Soda Muffins

Those of you who have tasted Irish soda bread know that it has a surprisingly delightful combination of flavors. The currants and light brown sugar provide a sweet accompaniment to the tangy buttermilk and citrus peel. And nestled right in the middle of it all is a fabulous zip of caraway seed. Mmm. Mmm.

I've spruced up the ingredients of traditional Irish soda bread by adding dark sweet cherries because they go so well with the orange and lemon. (Please read how to prepare the cherries under my Black Cherry Blossom Muffins on page 48.) And if you want to give the caraway seeds a burst of flavor, process them for a moment in your food processor or spice mill before adding them to the batter. I have also made these muffins with dried cherries, cranberries, blueberries, and raspberries. Delicious.

Dry Ingredients	Wet Ingredients
1½ cups unbleached white flour	1¼ cups nonfat buttermilk
1 cup whole-wheat flour	½ cup water
¼ cup light brown sugar	1 large egg
1 teaspoon baking powder	1 tablespoon grated orange peel
1 teaspoon baking soda	1 tablespoon grated lemon peel
¼ teaspoon sea salt	
1 tablespoon caraway seeds	

Goodies

½ cup dark sweet cherries, pitted and chopped
½ cup currants

Yield: 11–12 muffins

1. Preheat the oven to 400° F.

2. Sift all of the dry ingredients, except the caraway seeds, together in a large bowl. Add the caraway seeds and stir to combine. Add the goodies and toss to coat.

3. Whisk the wet ingredients in a medium bowl or blend them in your food processor. Pour the wet ingredients into the dry ingredients. Stir just until mixed. *Do not overstir.*

4. Spoon the batter into a greased or papered muffin tin. Fill each cup nearly to the top.

5. Bake for 15 to 20 minutes.

6. Cool the muffins at least 10 minutes before removing from the tin.

NUTRITIONAL FACTS (per 95-gram muffin)
Calories: 151 (5% from fat)

Fat: 1 g	Cholesterol: 19 mg	Carbohydrates: 32 g
Protein: 5 g	Fiber: 2.5 g	Sodium: 283 mg
Potassium: 195 mg	Iron: 1.5 mg	Calcium: 84 mg

Cranberry-Apple Muffins

Last Christmas, I made cranberry-apple conserve following a new recipe that my friend Nancy had given me during my Thanksgiving visit with her and her husband, Will. Everyone agreed that the conserve was a great new condiment for our holiday dinner, providing a delicious alternative to my usual cranberry-orange relish or Mom's cranberry sauce. I liked it so much I ate it every morning for a week with yogurt and a muffin.

Of course, my "muffin mind" saw the possibilities and I set about the task of creating this basic all-around muffin that you can enjoy for breakfast, dinner, or tea. I hope you like it.

Dry Ingredients	Wet Ingredients
1 cup whole-wheat pastry flour	1¼ cups nonfat buttermilk
¾ cup whole-wheat flour	½ cup apple juice
¾ cup unbleached white flour	½ cup honey
¼ cup light brown sugar	2 large egg whites
1 teaspoon baking powder	2 teaspoons grated orange peel
1 teaspoon baking soda	1 teaspoon rum extract
1 teaspoon ground cinnamon	
¼ teaspoon sea salt	

Goodies

1 medium apple, peeled and chopped (do not grate)
¾ cup dried cranberries

Yield: 12 muffins

1. Preheat the oven to 400° F.

2. Sift the dry ingredients together in a large bowl. Add the goodies and toss to coat.

3. Whisk the wet ingredients in a medium bowl or blend them in a food processor. Pour the wet ingredients into the dry mixture. Stir just until mixed. *Do not overstir.*

4. Spoon the batter into a greased or papered muffin tin. Fill each cup nearly to the top.

5. Bake for 15 to 20 minutes.

6. Cool the muffins at least 10 minutes before removing from the tin.

NUTRITIONAL FACTS (per 89-gram muffin)
Calories: 162 (2% from fat)

Fat: <1g	Cholesterol: <1mg	Carbohydrates: 38 g
Protein: 4 g	Fiber: 2.5 g	Sodium: 198 mg
Potassium: 205 mg	Iron: 1.2 mg	Calcium: 66 mg

Trust Your Own Experience

For me, the muffin-making process goes something like this:
I taste or read about or remember an interesting combina-
tion of flavors that I imagine would make a great muffin.
Then I prepare a first draft of a recipe and test it. Sometimes
I'm right on target and don't need to make any changes in
subsequent test runs. But other times, I'm way off.

When I made Catherine's Lemon Red Raspberry
Muffins (page 56) from my first-draft recipe, I followed
the usual procedure. I sifted the dry ingredients, added
and tossed the goodies, then blended the wet ingredients
in my food processor. But as I was about to pour the wet
ingredients into the dry mixture, I hesitated. There was a
gentle force preventing me from doing so. My instinct
told me there was too much liquid. If I used it all, the batter would be too runny and I would have to throw it out
and start all over again. Or I would have to compensate
for the excess liquid by adding more flour. Then, of
course, I would have to stir the batter too much and my
muffins would be rubbery and filled with holes.

For a few moments these thoughts ricocheted around
the inner walls of my brain. You know how it can be when
there are so many variables to consider in the moments
just before we act. One idea brings up a counter idea and

that, in turn, often brings us back to our original impulse.

In the end, my "what the heck" reflex won out and I poured the wet ingredients into the the dry ingredients.

The batter was too wet.

I had to add more flour and stir too much. And my muffins were rubbery and full of holes. In addition, the added stirring made the raspberries bleed into the batter so badly that the muffins were an unappealing purplish color instead of the light lemon yellow I had envisioned. I ended up throwing out the whole batch.

It's the same with writing. After working on this book's *Preface*, I was about to ask Rick, my writing partner, to read it. However, two sentences kept jumping off the page—they didn't seem right. I gave Rick the pages anyway. When he got back to me, he had flagged only two sentences. Yup. You know which ones.

The mistakes I have made while creating muffin recipes are the same ones I've made in life. And I think they are common human experiences. We don't always trust our own intuitive sense of what is right.

If, for one reason or another, you make changes in my recipes, or if you go wild and decide to create your own muffin recipes, do it! Trust your own sense of what is right and, if you are like me, over time you will notice a growing confidence in your own experience. And it will make you very happy.

Friends of the Earth Vegan Muffins

For several weeks, it seemed that every time I brought my muffins into the Friends of the Earth natural foods store where I sell them, the owners, Boyce and Tom asked me, "When are you gonna make us a vegan muffin?" Not being a vegan myself, I just never remembered to do it. And in all honesty, I think I privately believed that a vegan muffin simply wouldn't measure up to my strict taste standards.

I knew I could accomplish the task by substituting cornstarch for the eggs and eliminating dairy. But I couldn't make up my mind about the rest of the ingredients, so I asked Boyce and Tom. "If you could have anything you want in a vegan muffin, what would it be?" Without hesitation Boyce said it had to have walnuts, dates, and bananas.

As if to defy all of my earlier doubts, my Friends of the Earth Vegan Muffins were so successful that I tried substituting cornstarch for the egg in other recipes. I didn't retest all of my recipes, mind you, but I'm confident that you can substitute two tablespoons of cornstarch per egg (or per two egg whites) and fat-free soymilk for the cow's milk in any of my recipes to produce vegan muffins. Thus, you can make any of my muffins to suit your diet.

Dry Ingredients	Wet Ingredients
1¾ cups whole-wheat flour	2 ripe bananas, mashed
¾ cup whole-wheat pastry flour	(or 1 cup)
2 tablespoons cornstarch	1 cup fat-free soymilk
1½ teaspoons baking soda	½ cup honey
1 teaspoon baking powder	¼ cup apple-juice concentrate
1 teaspoon ground cinnamon	1 tablespoon molasses
¼ teaspoon sea salt	1 teaspoon vanilla extract
¼ teaspoon ground mace	1 teaspoon grated lemon rind

Goodies

½ cup coarsely chopped roasted walnuts (optional)
¼ cup chopped dates
¼ cup dried fruit bits

Yield: 12 muffins

1. Preheat the oven to 400° F.

2. Sift the dry ingredients together in a large bowl.

3. Whisk the wet ingredients in a medium bowl or blend them in a food processor. Add the goodies and stir to combine.

4. Pour the wet mixture into the dry ingredients. Stir just until mixed. *Do not overstir.*

5. Spoon the batter into a greased or papered muffin tin. Fill each cup nearly to the top.

6. Bake for 15 to 20 minutes.

7. Cool the muffins at least 10 minutes before removing from the tin.

NUTRITIONAL FACTS (per 95-gram muffin without walnuts)
Calories: 193 (3% from fat)

Fat: 1 g	Cholesterol: 0 mg	Carbohydrates: 47 g
Protein: 4 g	Fiber: 4.0 g	Sodium: 235 mg
Potassium: 304 mg	Iron: 1.5 mg	Calcium: 83 mg

NUTRITIONAL FACTS (per 100-gram muffin with walnuts)
Calories: 226 (15% from fat)

Fat: 4 g	Cholesterol: 0 mg	Carbohydrates: 48 g
Protein: 5 g	Fiber: 4.2 g	Sodium: 236 mg
Potassium: 329 mg	Iron: 1.7 mg	Calcium: 88

Lemon-Yogurt Poppy-Seed Muffins

I used to think that poppy-seed cakes and breads were the brain children of coffee-house patrons or dessert connoisseurs, who recognized their undisputed place alongside such offerings as pound cake, cheesecake, and French pastries. But the use of poppy seeds in baked goods is not a contemporary innovation. It goes back as far as ancient Greece and Asia. Maybe that's why most people enjoy them so much. By now, our pleasure is probably genetically determined.

Contrary to what you may have heard, poppy seeds have no narcotic properties. It is true that they are derived from the opium poppy plant, but the seeds form only after the narcotic properties of the plant have come and gone.

Dry Ingredients	Wet Ingredients
1 cup whole-wheat flour	1 cup skim milk
1 cup unbleached white flour	¼ cup plain nonfat yogurt
¼ cup brown rice flour	¼ cup honey
½ cup light brown sugar	1 large egg
1 teaspoon baking powder	3 tablespoons grated lemon peel
1 teaspoon baking soda	1 teaspoon vanilla extract
¼ teaspoon sea salt	
2 tablespoons poppy seeds	

Yield: 12 muffins

1. Preheat the oven to 375° F.

2. Sift all of the dry ingredients, except the poppy seeds, together in a large bowl. Add the poppy seeds and stir to combine.

3. Whisk the wet ingredients in a medium bowl or blend them in a food processor. Pour the wet ingredients into the dry ingredients. Stir until mixed. *Do not overstir.*

4. Spoon the batter into a greased or papered muffin tin. Fill each cup nearly to the top.

5. Bake for 15 to 20 minutes.

6. Cool the muffins at least 10 minutes before removing from the tin.

NUTRITIONAL FACTS (per 83-gram muffin)
Calories: 165 (8% from fat)

Fat: 1 g	Cholesterol: 18mg	Carbohydrates: 35 g
Protein: 5 g	Fiber: 2.1 g	Sodium: 200 mg
Potassium: 217 mg	Iron: 1.3 mg	Calcium: 121 mg

Maple (Pecan) Muffins

Barley flour does funny things to batter. It's heavy and tends to pull the rest of the ingredients down. So, you may find that this batter is a little flat. Don't be alarmed. Like a good romance novel, everything comes out all right in the end.

For a dessert-y treat, try topping these muffins with a no-fat maple cream-cheese icing. Simply whip 4 ounces of fat-free cream cheese with 2 tablespoons of maple syrup. After the muffins have completely cooled, spread a spoonful of icing on each.

For an even lower-fat version of this muffin, exclude the pecans. This will reduce the fat content from 4 grams to 1 per muffin.

Dry Ingredients	Wet Ingredients
¾ cup whole-wheat pastry flour	1 cup maple syrup
½ cup whole-wheat flour	¾ cup skim milk
½ cup unbleached white flour	2 large egg whites
½ cup barley flour	
¼ cup malted milk powder	
1½ teaspoons baking powder	
½ teaspoon baking soda	
¼ teaspoon sea salt	

Goodies

½ cup chopped roasted pecans (optional)

FRESH & FRUITY, SOMETIMES NUTTY MUFFINS

Yield: 11–12 muffins

1. Preheat the oven to 400° F.

2. Sift the dry ingredients together in a large bowl. Add the pecans (if using) and toss to coat.

3. Whisk the wet ingredients in a medium bowl or blend them in a food processor. Pour the wet ingredients into the dry mixture. Stir just until mixed. *Do not overstir.*

4. Spoon the batter into a greased or papered muffin tin. Fill each cup nearly to the top.

5. Bake for 15 to 20 minutes.

6. Cool the muffins at least 10 minutes before removing from the tin.

NUTRITIONAL FACTS (per 73-gram muffin without pecans)
Calories: 169 (4% from fat)

Fat: 1 g	Cholesterol: 1 mg	Carbohydrates: 37 g
Protein: 4 g	Fiber: 2.1 g	Sodium: 176 mg
Potassium: 211 mg	Iron: 1.0 mg	Calcium: 100 mg

NUTRITIONAL FACTS (per 78-gram muffin with pecans)
Calories: 200 (17% from fat)

Fat: 4 g	Cholesterol: 1 mg	Carbohydrates: 39 g
Protein: 5 g	Fiber: 2.4 g	Sodium: 176 mg
Potassium: 229 mg	Iron: 1.2 mg	Calcium: 102 mg

Mom's Applesauce Muffins

*I reincarnated this recipe from my first cookbook, **Gloria's Glorious Muffins**.
It's one of the recipes that I seem to go back to over and over again. And it's one
of my most frequently requested muffins. In the interest of making this version
even more attractive than the original, I made a few changes. I took out the nuts,
lightened the batter a bit by using unbleached white flour, and replaced the apple-
juice concentrate (which I think caused the muffins to burn easily) with more
applesauce and a little light brown sugar. These changes reduced the fat content
from the original 6 grams per muffin to 1 gram.*

*The Vanilla Yogurt-Cheese Icing used with the Standard Spice Muffins on page
224, is perfect with these muffins. And it won't increase the fat content at all.*

Dry Ingredients	Wet Ingredients
1½ cups whole-wheat pastry flour	1 cup chunky applesauce
½ cup whole-wheat flour	¾ cup skim milk
½ cup unbleached white flour	½ cup water
½ cup light brown sugar	1 large egg
2½ teaspoons baking powder	
1 teaspoon cocoa powder	
1 teaspoon ground cinnamon	
½ teaspoon ground nutmeg	
½ teaspoon ground allspice	
¼ teaspoon sea salt	

Goodies

¾ cup raisins
¾ cup chopped dates

Yield: 12 muffins

1. Preheat the oven to 400° F.

2. Sift the dry ingredients together in a large bowl.

3. Whisk the wet ingredients in a medium bowl or blend them in a food processor. Add the goodies and stir to combine.

4. Pour the wet mixture into the dry ingredients. Stir just until mixed. *Do not overstir.*

5. Spoon the batter into a greased or papered muffin tin. Fill each cup nearly to the top.

6. Bake for 15 to 20 minutes.

7. Cool the muffins at least 10 minutes before removing from the tin.

NUTRITIONAL FACTS (per 95-gram muffin)
Calories: 194 (4% from fat)

Fat: 1 g	Cholesterol: 18 mg	Carbohydrates: 45 g
Protein: 4 g	Fiber: 3.7 g	Sodium: 130 mg
Potassium: 329 mg	Iron: 1.7 mg	Calcium: 126 mg

Orange-Strawberry-Banana Muffins

Fresh strawberries just don't hold up in muffins. If you cut them into bite-sized pieces, they turn to mush as the muffins bake and the batter around the bits of strawberry becomes spongy and gooey. If you purée the fresh strawberries, the muffins will have a funny color—sort of purplish brown. Very unappetizing. And, too, the strawberry flavor just doesn't come through. I know this. I have made muffins with fresh strawberries before.

So why did I use chopped fresh strawberries when I first made my Orange-Strawberry-Banana Muffins? Why did I think it wouldn't happen this time, that this time it would be different? Sometimes we humans just don't have confidence in our own good sense and experience, do we? Or we forget, or something. Then we have to go back and learn things over again.

Anyway, these muffins are made with strawberry flavoring instead of fresh strawberries. Take my word for it . . . or learn it for yourself.

Dry Ingredients	Wet Ingredients
1 cup whole-wheat flour	2 ripe bananas, mashed
1 cup unbleached white flour	(or 1 cup)
½ cup light brown sugar	1 cup skim milk
1 teaspoon baking powder	2 large egg whites
1 teaspoon baking soda	1 tablespoon strawberry
½ cup ground nutmeg	flavoring
¼ teaspoon sea salt	1 tablespoon grated orange peel
½ cup oat bran	1 teaspoon vanilla extract

Yield: 12 muffins

1. Preheat the oven to 375° F.

2. Sift all of the dry ingredients, except the oat bran, together in a large bowl. Add the oat bran and stir to combine.

3. Whisk the wet ingredients in a medium bowl or blend them in a food processor. Pour the wet ingredients into the dry mixture. Stir just until mixed. *Do not overstir.*

4. Spoon the batter into a greased or papered muffin tin. Fill each cup nearly to the top.

5. Bake for 15 to 20 minutes.

6. Cool the muffins at least 10 minutes before removing from the tin.

NUTRITIONAL FACTS (per 94-gram muffin)
Calories: 167 (5% from fat)

Fat: 1 g	Cholesterol: <1 mg	Carbohydrates: 38 g
Protein: 5 g	Fiber: 2.9 g	Sodium: 230 mg
Potassium: 305 mg	Iron: 1.5 mg	Calcium: 83 mg

Pumpkin-Banana Muffins

Last fall, my friend Susan gave me half of a huge pumpkin that a neighbor had grown and given to her. Susan had exhausted her pumpkin recipe repertoire and still had half of the pumpkin left. Sure, you can always steam, purée, and freeze it, but we agreed that when you get a fresh home-grown pumpkin, you should honor it and the person who grew it by using it while it is fresh.

Now it was my turn to go pumpkin crazy. I made pumpkin-and-beer soup, pumpkin yeast bread, and pumpkin stew. And I still had a few cups of pumpkin purée left. As I sat in the kitchen paging through my cookbooks in search of new ideas, the phone rang. It was Sydney and Meredith inviting me over for dinner. "Great," I said, "What can I bring?" They suggested something for dessert. Something sweet.

And that is how I stumbled upon a fabulous pumpkin-banana custard recipe. I made it. We ate it. We drooled. And from that dessert, the idea for my Pumpkin-Banana Muffins was born.

Dry Ingredients	Wet Ingredients
1 cup whole-wheat flour	2 ripe bananas, mashed
1 cup unbleached white flour	(or 1 cup)
½ cup brown rice flour	1 cup pumpkin purée
¾ cup light brown sugar	1 cup skim milk
1½ teaspoons baking soda	2 large egg whites
1 teaspoon baking powder	1 teaspoon grated lemon peel
2 teaspoons ground cinnamon	
1 teaspoon ground nutmeg	
¼ teaspoon sea salt	

Yield: 12 muffins

1. Preheat the oven to 375° F.

2. Sift the dry ingredients together in a large bowl.

3. Whisk the wet ingredients in a medium bowl or blend them in a food processor. Pour the wet ingredients into the dry ingredients. Stir just until mixed. *Do not overstir.*

4. Spoon the batter into a greased or papered muffin tin. Fill each cup nearly to the top.

5. Bake for 15 to 20 minutes.

6. Cool the muffins at least 10 minutes before removing from the tin.

NUTRITIONAL FACTS (per 107-gram muffin)
Calories: 180 (3% from fat)

Fat: 1 g	Cholesterol: <1 mg	Carbohydrates: 41 g
Protein: 5 g	Fiber: 2.8 g	Sodium: 248 mg
Potassium: 308 mg	Iron: 1.7 mg	Calcium: 83 mg

3.

CRUNCHY, CRUMBLY, SPICY DO-DA MUFFINS

The idea for this selection of gourmet muffins grew out of a simple observation. I've noticed that whenever I enter a room with a basketful of muffins—whether to sell them at Friends of the Earth or to offer them at a party or pot-luck meal—people automatically reach for the muffins with interesting crunchy or crumbly toppings.

"Ooo! What's that one?"

"Save me one with the stuff on top."

Granted, they are also interested in knowing whether any of the muffins in my basket contain chocolate. But that's another story and why I wrote Chapter Five.

The topping doesn't have to be anything particularly complicated. A pinch of nuts or seeds, a sprinkling of toasted wheat germ, or a shred of coconut will do. The point is that, more often than not, the crunchy, crumbly muffins are the first ones to go.

This is an interesting phenomenon, one that I fully understand. When ordering a meal at a restaurant or flipping through my cookbooks, I find I am usually most interested in the entrées that are smothered in a sauce or perhaps topped with a sprinkling of cheese. Given the option, I pick crumb cake over pound cake every time. And muffins with appealing crunchy, crumbly toppings are hard to resist. I think we like having a little something extra to make what we eat look special. And why not?

The only thing that can draw my attention away from the lure of crumbly toppings is spice. It tingles my taste buds. In fact, if you ask me which muffins are my favorites, I'd say the ones with lots of spice.

So here's a chapter with everybody's favorites—"Crunchy, Crumbly, Spicy Do-Da Muffins." What a mouthful! And are they ever!

Almond Cardamom Fig Muffins

Dried figs are surprisingly high in fiber—2.6 grams per ounce, compared to 1.1 grams in raisins and 2 grams in prunes. They are "good for what ails you," as the saying goes.

After learning these fiber facts, I decided to create a fig muffin. At first, I wasn't sure I'd be happy with the results. I mean, if you bite into a particularly seedy dried fig it can feel as though you've lost a filling and have crushed it to bits between your twelve-year molars, or as though the molecules of your body are breaking up and preparing to be teleported through cyberspace. But the idea of creating a muffin with so much fiber was too attractive to pass up.

With 5.3 grams of fiber each, my Almond Cardamom Fig Muffins are among the highest-fiber muffins I make. Other muffins that are particularly high in fiber are Apple-iscious Apple Spice (page 88), Better Banana (Nut) Bran (page 46), Friends of the Earth Vegan (page 64), Toasted Wheat Germ Crunch (page 110), and Prune Spice (page 108).

Dry Ingredients	Wet Ingredients
1½ cups whole-wheat flour	1¾ cups skim milk
1 cup unbleached white flour	¾ cup applesauce
¼ cup sugar	1 large egg
1 teaspoon baking powder	1½ teaspoons almond extract
1 teaspoon baking soda	½ teaspoon vanilla extract
½ teaspoon ground cardamom	
¼ teaspoon sea salt	

Goodies

1 cup chopped dried figs
½ cup sliced almonds

Yield: 11–12 muffins

1. Preheat the oven to 400° F.

2. Sift the dry ingredients together in a large bowl. Add the figs and toss to coat.

3. Whisk the wet ingredients in a medium bowl or blend them in a food processor. Pour the wet ingredients into the dry mixture. Stir just until mixed. *Do not overstir.*

4. Spoon the batter into a greased or papered muffin tin. Fill each cup nearly to the top. Top each cup of batter with a large pinch of sliced almonds, taking care to sprinkle them evenly over each cup.

5. Bake for 15 to 20 minutes.

6. Cool the muffins at least 10 minutes before removing from the tin.

NUTRITIONAL FACTS (per 114-gram muffin)
Calories: 229 (14% from fat)

Fat: 3 g	Cholesterol: 22 mg	Carbohydrates: 45 g
Protein: 7 g	Fiber: 5.3 g	Sodium: 234 mg
Potassium: 392 mg	Iron: 2.0 mg	Calcium: 138 mg

Almond Delight Muffins

Try eating an almond (only one at a time, please) like this: First, clear your palate with a little iced tea, lemonade, or perhaps a splash of white wine. Then place the almond between your back teeth and bite down a few times until you sense the almond flavor throughout your mouth. Roll your tongue around the broken bits of almond and let your taste buds do their thing. Now describe what you feel, taste, sense.

It's amazing. When the flavor bursts forth in my mouth, I feel a warm, almost numbing sensation in my throat and neck area. I notice that I'm suddenly more relaxed and I breathe more deeply, as if I am soaking in a bath of warm milk. Warm and soothing—that's what I should have called these muffins.

Almond Delight Muffins derive 18 percent of their calories from fat. That's high compared to most of the muffins in this book. But before you decide to skip this recipe, consider the following fact. Muffins containing nuts are high in protein, fiber, and other essential nutrients. For more information on nuts, see Crazy About Nuts and Seeds beginning on page 82.

Dry Ingredients	Wet Ingredients
1½ cups whole-wheat pastry flour	1 cup skim milk
1 cup whole-wheat flour	¾ cup nonfat sour cream
½ cup unbleached white flour	2 large egg whites
1½ teaspoons baking powder	1½ teaspoons almond extract
½ teaspoon ground ginger	1 teaspoon vanilla extract
½ teaspoon ground cinnamon	
½ teaspoon ground nutmeg	
¼ teaspoon sea salt	

Goodies

¾ cup dark brown sugar
½ cup coarsely chopped almonds

Yield: 12 muffins

1. Preheat the oven to 400° F.

2. Sift the dry ingredients together in a large bowl.

3. Combine the goodies in a separate bowl. Reserve ½ cup of this goody mixture to top the muffins (see Step 5). Add the remaining mixture to the dry ingredients and stir to combine.

4. Whisk the wet ingredients in a medium bowl or blend them in a food processor. Pour the wet ingredients into the dry mixture. Stir just until mixed. *Do not overstir.*

5. Spoon the batter into a greased or papered muffin tin. Fill each cup nearly to the top. Top each cup of batter with the remaining brown sugar-and-almond goody mixture, taking care to sprinkle it evenly over each cup.

6. Bake for 15 to 20 minutes.

7. Cool the muffins at least 10 minutes before removing from the tin.

NUTRITIONAL FACTS (per 84-gram muffin)
Calories: 186 (18% from fat)

Fat: 3 g	Cholesterol: <1 mg	Carbohydrates: 33 g
Protein: 7 g	Fiber: 3.1 g	Sodium: 123 mg
Potassium: 272 mg	Iron: 1.4 mg	Calcium: 119 mg

Crazy About Nuts and Seeds

One can hardly write a low-fat muffin cookbook without discussing nuts and seeds and their relatively high-fat content. Seen from one perspective, if you're cutting back on dietary fat it would make sense to reduce your intake of nuts and seeds. With the exception of chestnuts, which contain less than 1 gram of fat per ounce and derive only 8 percent of their calories from fat, most nuts and seeds contain 15 to 20 grams of fat per ounce and derive more than 75 percent of their calories from fat. (*See* Table 3.1 Calorie, Fat, and Cholesterol Content of Nuts and Seeds, on pages 84–85.)

Fortunately, nothing in life is ever that simple and there are a number of other factors to consider when deciding what to do about nuts and seeds. For one thing, it is important to understand that the fats contained in most nuts and seeds are almost entirely monounsaturated and polyunsaturated—the so-called good fats. (For further information on the different types of fat, see discussion beginning on page 30.) This means that nuts and seeds do not contain much saturated fat, which has been associated with heart disease, high cholesterol levels, and high blood pressure. In fact, unsaturated fats like the kind found in nuts and seeds have been shown to *lower* these health risks. A study on macadamia nuts, for example, indicated that these nuts actually help lower blood pressure and reduce cholesterol. And other studies have shown that eating nuts may lower the level of fatty substances that clog the arteries.

Besides, nuts and seeds contain important nutrients. They are an excellent source of protein, fiber, calcium, and magnesium. Some nuts and seeds supply vitamin E. Linoleic acid, a polyunsaturated fat that is found in nuts and seeds, is essential for life.

Does this mean that we can gobble up nuts and seeds by the handful? No. But it does mean that eating an ounce of nuts or seeds is not the same as eating an ounce of butter. We need some fats in our diet, and nuts and seeds—basic and natural foods—are good sources of that fat.

Because I recognize that some people may wish to limit their intake of nuts, in most cases I have made them optional. For those muffins in which the nuts are optional, the name of the nut appears in parentheses in the recipe title. You can leave the nuts out of such recipes and still end up with fabulous muffins. In other recipes, the nuts are not optional—they are necessary for the muffin's success.

When deciding what to do about nuts and seeds, remember this—nearly all of my muffins contain only 3 grams of fat or less. And all but one of my muffins made with nuts contain only 4 grams of fat. Now that's something to go nuts about!

Table 3.1 Calorie, Fat, and Cholesterol Content of Nuts and Seeds

The nutritional analysis of the following is based on 1-ounce servings.

Product	Calories	Total Fat gms	Percent of Fat Calories %
Almonds, dry roasted *	166	15	80
Brazil nuts	186	19	91
Cashews, dry roasted	163	13	73
Chestnuts, roasted	69	1	8
Filberts, dry roasted	188	19	90
Macadamia nuts, oil roasted	204	22	96
Peanuts, dry roasted**	166	14	76
Pecans	187	18	88
Pine nuts	146	14	89
Pistachios	172	15	78
Poppy seeds	151	13	75
Pumpkin seeds	148	12	73
Sesame seeds	167	16	84
Sunflower seeds	175	16	83
Walnuts	182	18	87

*   An almond is actually not a nut. It is a stone fruit and is related to the plum and peach.

**   Peanuts are actually legumes, not nuts.

Saturated Fat gms	Monounsaturated Fat gms	Polyunsaturated Fat gms	Cholesterol gms
1	10	3	0
5	7	7	0
3	8	2	0
<1	<1	<1	0
1	15	2	0
3	17	<1	0
2	7	4	0
1	11	5	0
2	5	6	0
2	10	2	0
1	2	9	0
2	4	5	0
<1	<1	<1	0
2	3	11	0
2	4	11	0

Apple (Walnut) Crumble Muffins

I held a Sunday breakfast in honor of my nephew Rick, who had just graduated from The North Carolina School of the Arts as an accomplished actor. A number of my friends joined me to bid Rick farewell as he prepared to leave for New York City. I am sure I could have served tea and toast, as our attention was clearly on Rick. But instead I served my Apple (Walnut) Crumble Muffins with fresh fruit and coffee.

In the years to come we may forget exactly which muffins I served that day, but we will never forget the good feelings that they helped create.

Dry Ingredients	Wet Ingredients
1 cup whole-wheat flour	1¼ cups nonfat buttermilk
1 cup unbleached white flour	¾ cup applesauce
1 teaspoon baking powder	½ cup honey
1 teaspoon baking soda	2 large egg whites
1 teaspoon ground cinnamon	1 teaspoon vanilla extract
½ teaspoon ground ginger	
¼ teaspoon sea salt	

Goodies

1 medium apple, peeled and chopped (do not grate)
1 cup chopped roasted walnuts (optional)

Crumble Topping

½ cup unbleached white flour
¼ cup light brown sugar
½ teaspoon ground cinnamon
1 tablespoon light margarine, softened to room temperature.

Yield: 12 muffins

1. Preheat the oven to 400° F.

2. Prepare the crumble topping by combining the flour, brown sugar, and cinnamon in a medium bowl. Using a pastry blender or two knives, cut the margarine into this mixture to form a crumbly topping. Set aside.

3. Sift the dry ingredients together in a large bowl. Add the goodies and toss to coat.

4. Whisk the wet ingredients in a medium bowl or blend them in a food processor. Pour the wet ingredients into the dry mixture. Stir just until mixed. *Do not overstir.*

5. Spoon the batter into a greased or papered muffin tin. Fill each cup nearly to the top. Top each cup of batter with the crumble topping, taking care to spread it evenly over each cup. Too much topping piled in the middle will prevent the muffins from rising properly.

6. Bake for 15 to 20 minutes.

7. Cool the muffins at least 10 minutes before removing from the tin.

NUTRITIONAL FACTS (per 82-gram muffin without walnuts)
Calories: 167 (6% from fat)

Fat: 1 g	Cholesterol: 0 mg	Carbohydrates: 37 g
Protein: 4 g	Fiber: 2.1 g	Sodium: 210 mg
Potassium: 134 mg	Iron: 1.2 mg	Calcium: 63 mg

NUTRITIONAL FACTS (per 90-gram muffin with walnuts)
Calories: 234 (28% from fat)

Fat: 7 g	Cholesterol: 0 mg	Carbohydrates: 38 g
Protein: 6 g	Fiber: 2.5 g	Sodium: 211 mg
Potassium: 185 mg	Iron: 1.4 mg	Calcium: 72 mg

Apple-iscious
Apple Spice Muffins

It's not easy to find words that aptly describe a taste. You know how it is. Naming belongs to a sort of cognitive brain function while tasting is definitely sensual; and the effort to communicate sensation with words almost always falls short of the mark. But the name for these muffins is pretty darn close to the sensation you'll experience while enjoying them. Say it and sense it—these muffins are apple-iscious!

I think my Apple-iscious Apple Spice Muffins are plenty sweet without the added sugar, but one of my taste testers feels they need more. I suggest trying them first without the sugar. If you feel they aren't sweet enough, add the sugar next time.

Dry Ingredients	Wet Ingredients
1 cup whole-wheat pastry flour	1½ cups water
1 cup whole-wheat flour	1 cup applesauce
½ cup barley flour	¼ cup apple butter
¼ cup sugar (optional)	1 large egg
1½ teaspoons baking soda	2 teaspoons grated lemon peel
1 teaspoon baking powder	1 teaspoon vanilla extract
¼ teaspoon ground nutmeg	
¼ teaspoon sea salt	

Goodies

2 medium apples, peeled and chopped (do not grate)

Crunchy Topping

½ cup honey crunch wheat germ
¼ cup light brown sugar

Yield: 12 muffins

1. Preheat the oven to 400° F.

2. Prepare the crunchy topping by combining the wheat germ and brown sugar in a small bowl. Set aside.

3. Sift the dry ingredients together in a large bowl. Add the apples and toss to coat.

4. Whisk the wet ingredients in a medium bowl or blend them in a food processor. Pour the wet ingredients into the dry mixture. Stir just until mixed. *Do not overstir.*

5. Spoon the batter into a greased or papered muffin tin. Fill each cup nearly to the top. Generously top each cup of batter with the crunchy topping, taking care to spread it evenly over each cup.

6. Bake for 15 to 20 minutes.

7. Cool the muffins for at least 10 minutes before removing from the tin.

NUTRITIONAL FACTS (per 106-gram muffin)
Calories: 158 (7% from fat)

Fat: 1 g	Cholesterol: 18 mg	Carbohydrates: 34 g
Protein: 5 g	Fiber: 4.1 g	Sodium: 229 mg
Potassium: 216 mg	Iron: 1.3 mg	Calcium: 46 mg

Apricot Sesame Muffins

I never liked apricots. Every Christmas when I was a kid my family received a gift crate of dried fruits from California (I think) that was sent by one of the vendors with whom my dad did business. My sister Marlene always hogged the apricots. She thought they were great. Me? They made my lips pucker. "Marlene can have those silly apricots," I thought. "They're more sour than grapefruit!"

I was in my mid-twenties before I opened up to apricots. I tried a fresh one and was surprised to discover that apricots aren't sour at all—at least when they are fresh and ripe. Drying seems to sharpen their flavor, making them tart. These Apricot Sesame Muffins are an effort to bring the sweetness of apricots together with their sharpness. To this I've added a light sprinkling of sesame seeds. It was a good idea. You'll see.

Dry Ingredients	Wet Ingredients
1 cup unbleached white flour	¾ cup buttermilk
¾ cup whole-wheat pastry flour	1 large egg
½ cup brown rice flour	1 teaspoon vanilla extract
½ cup light brown sugar	
1 teaspoon baking powder	
1 teaspoon baking soda	
¼ teaspoon sea salt	

Goodies

1 cup chopped dried apricots

16-ounce can apricots packed in fruit juice, well drained

Topping

3 tablespoons sesame seeds

Yield: 11–12 muffins

1. Preheat the oven to 400° F.

2. Sift the dry ingredients together in a large bowl. Add the dried apricots and toss to coat.

3. Purée the canned apricots in a food processor or blender to yield about 1 cup purée. Add the wet ingredients and pulse to blend. (You can also use a fork or potato ricer to mash the apricots, then blend in the wet ingredients by hand.)

4. Pour the wet mixture into the dry mixture. Stir just until mixed. *Do not overstir.*

5. Spoon the batter into a greased or papered muffin tin. Fill each cup nearly to the top. Top each cup of batter with a large pinch of sesame seeds, taking care to sprinkle them evenly over each cup.

6. Bake for 15 to 20 minutes.

7. Cool the muffins at least 10 minutes before removing from the tin.

NUTRITIONAL FACTS (per 113-gram muffin)
Calories: 188 (10% from fat)

Fat: 2 g	Cholesterol: 19 mg	Carbohydrates: 39 g
Protein: 5 g	Fiber: 2.8 g	Sodium: 226 mg
Potassium: 359 mg	Iron: 1.9 mg	Calcium: 94 mg

Blueberries, Oats, and Cream Muffins, Too

This recipe may sound familiar. I offered you Blueberries, Oats, and Cream Muffins in Chapter 2. I make these muffins two different ways and couldn't decide which of the versions I liked best, so I included them both. This version has the added flavor of barley flour and malted milk. It also has a wonderful oat-and-brown-sugar crumble topping. Try both recipes to see which muffin you like better!

Dry Ingredients	Wet Ingredients
1 cup whole-wheat flour	1 cup nonfat sour cream
1 cup unbleached white flour	¾ cup apple juice
¼ cup barley flour	½ cup water
¼ cup malted milk powder	½ cup honey
1½ teaspoons baking soda	1 large egg
1 teaspoon baking powder	2 teaspoons grated orange peel
¼ teaspoon sea salt	1 teaspoon vanilla extract
¼ cup rolled oats	

Goodies

³/₄ cup firm fresh blueberries, washed and patted dry

Crumble Topping

1 tablespoon whole-wheat flour	¼ cup rolled oats
1 tablespoon unbleached white flour	½ teaspoon ground cinnamon
¼ cup light brown sugar	2 tablespoons margarine, softened to room temperature

Yield: 12 muffins

1. Preheat the oven to 375° F.

2. Prepare the crumble topping by combining the flours, brown sugar, oats, and cinnamon in a medium bowl. Using a pastry blender or two knives, cut the margarine into this mixture to form a crumbly topping. Set aside.

3. Sift all of the dry ingredients, except the oats, together in a large bowl. Add the oats and stir to combine. Add the blueberries and toss to coat.

4. Whisk the wet ingredients in a medium bowl or blend them in a food processor. Pour the wet ingredients into the dry mixture. Stir just until mixed. *Do not overstir.*

5. Spoon the batter into a greased or papered muffin tin. Fill each cup nearly to the top. Top each cup of batter with the crumble topping, taking care to spread it evenly over each cup. Too much topping piled in the middle will prevent the muffins from rising properly.

6. Bake for 15 to 20 minutes.

7. Cool the muffins at least 10 minutes before removing from the tin.

NUTRITIONAL FACTS (per 113-gram muffin)
Calories: 224 (11% from fat)

Fat: 3 g	Cholesterol: 19 mg	Carbohydrates: 45 g
Protein: 6 g	Fiber: 2.7 g	Sodium: 295 mg
Potassium: 244 mg	Iron: 1.4 mg	Calcium: 80 mg

Café Crumble Muffins

Following the completion of an extensive retreat at a Buddhist monastery in England, I took a taxi into Hemel Hempstead to catch the bus to Heathrow airport. Having arrived at the bus station with time to spare, I checked my bags and walked up the alley to a bakery where the aroma of fresh-baked pastries overcame my senses.

"What's in that one?" I asked the woman at the counter as I pointed to a rather plain looking, tube-shaped cake with a buttery crumble topping.

"It's coffee cake, Deary," replied the no-longer middle-aged attendant. She wore a starched apron and cap that reminded me of a French maid.

Sounding very American and feeling alien to England and Her ways (in spite of the three half-frozen months I had just spent there), I asked, "Do you mean it contains coffee or that it is to be enjoyed with coffee?"

The woman looked so puzzled at my query that I decided to spare her the unpleasantness of having to respond to what was obviously a clash of cultures. "Never mind," I interrupted her pause. "I'll take a slice."

The coffee cake was delightful. To this day I don't know the answer to my question, but it doesn't matter. The cake with its crumble topping and the matron behind the counter inspired my Café Crumble Muffins. The yogurt gives the muffins a bit of tang that is complimented nicely by the sweet crumbly topping.

Dry Ingredients	Wet Ingredients
1½ cups unbleached white flour	¾ cup triple-strength coffee,
1 cup whole-wheat flour	cooled to room temperature
¼ cup light brown sugar	½ cup plain nonfat yogurt
1½ teaspoons baking soda	½ cup honey
1 teaspoon baking powder	2 large egg whites
¼ teaspoon sea salt	1 ½ teaspoons vanilla extract

Crumble Topping

¼ cup unbleached white flour

⅛ cup whole-wheat flour

3 tablespoons dark brown sugar

2 tablespoons light margarine, softened to room temperature

Yield: 11–12 muffins

1. Preheat the oven to 400° F.

2. Prepare the crumble topping by combining the flours and brown sugar in a medium bowl. Using a pastry blender or two knives, cut the margarine into the mixture to form a crumbly topping. Set aside.

3. Sift the dry ingredients together in a large bowl.

4. Whisk the wet ingredients in a medium bowl or blend them in a food processor. Pour the wet ingredients into the dry ingredients. Stir just until mixed. *Do not overstir.*

5. Spoon the batter into a greased or papered muffin tin. Fill each cup nearly to the top. Top each cup of batter with the crumble topping, taking care to spread it evenly over each cup. Too much topping piled in the middle will prevent the muffins from rising properly.

6. Bake for 15 to 20 minutes.

7. Cool the muffins at least 10 minutes before removing from the tin.

NUTRITIONAL FACTS (per 73-gram muffin)
Calories: 204 (8% from fat)

Fat: 2 g	Cholesterol: <1 mg	Carbohydrates: 43 g
Protein: 5 g	Fiber: 2.1 g	Sodium: 275 mg
Potassium: 186 mg	Iron: 1.5 mg	Calcium: 63 mg

Eat No Muffin Before Its Time

Sascha is always excited to see me. When I drive into the backyard, she races back and forth, back and forth within the walls of the chain-link fence that frames her territory—all the while howling and barking and letting the entire neighborhood know that I've returned. If I spend too much time gathering my things before getting out of the car, Sascha goes bananas. She's got so much stored-up energy that she can't bear to wait another second before giving me a smooch and letting me stroke her belly. She is impatience on four legs and covered in fur.

When it comes time to enjoy my muffins, however, Sascha puts on another face. While I am certain she has no real understanding of time and calendars and schedules, when I enter the kitchen each Thursday morning, I believe Sascha knows it's baking day and she becomes the mistress of forbearance. Like a centurion patiently guarding his post, Sascha assumes her position in the back foyer at the bottom of the stairs. From this vantage point, she can see my every move and is ready to jump up the instant I reach for her bowl to give her a freshly baked muffin. Until that time, she waits, waits, waits, all morning long—stirring only to guard me against the letter carrier, sanitation workers, or other "threatening" outsiders.

Given her obvious love of muffins, one would guess that when the muffin finally appears in her bowl, she would wolf it down with a passion. Most of the time she does just that. However, I've noticed that if I offer her a muffin before it is fully cooled, she sniffs it, looks at me a bit puzzled, sniffs it again, and walks away. In a few minutes, she returns to check the fare. If it is cool enough, she devours it in her usual style.

I find this an amazing display of wisdom and self-control. When it comes to eating muffins, Sascha has more sense than I do. It took me several bellyaches from eating muffins that were too hot before I finally learned what Sascha instinctively knew—that muffins just don't settle right in the stomach unless they have been fully cooled first. No matter how wonderful the anticipated pleasure, she waits and waits and eats no muffin before its time.

Coco Nana Muffins

Are you surprised to see a low-fat muffin recipe that calls for coconut? Don't be. Coconut is not the problem you may think it is. This recipe calls for only ¾ cup of standard flaked coconut, half of which is used to top the muffins. The muffins look inviting and each delicious bite is filled with coconut flavor.

Of the 3 grams of fat in each of these muffins, 2 come from the coconut. To me, that's worth it. If, however, you want to reduce the fat grams to less than 2 per muffin, eliminate the coconut from the batter and use only ⅜ cup as topping. You can also eliminate the coconut altogether and add 1½ teaspoons coconut flavoring to the wet ingredients. Then your Coco Nana Muffins will be nearly fat-free.

Note: When you reduce the ingredients in any recipe, remember that the yield will likewise be reduced.

Dry Ingredients	Wet Ingredients
1½ cups whole-wheat flour	3 ripe bananas, mashed
1 cup unbleached white flour	(or 1½ cups)
½ cup light brown sugar	1 cup skim milk
1½ teaspoons baking powder	¼ cup orange-juice concentrate
1 teaspoon baking soda	1 large egg
¼ teaspoon sea salt	1 tablespoon grated orange peel
¾ cup flaked coconut	1 teaspoon vanilla extract
	1 teaspoon rum flavoring

Yield: 11–12 muffins

1. Preheat the oven to 375° F.

2. Sift all of the dry ingredients, except the coconut, together in a large bowl. Reserve ⅜ cup of the coconut to top the muffins (see Step 4). Add the remaining coconut to the dry ingredients and stir to combine.

3. Whisk the wet ingredients in a medium bowl or blend them in a food processor. Pour the wet ingredients into the dry ingredients. Stir just until mixed. *Do not overstir.*

4. Spoon the batter into a greased or papered muffin tin. Fill each cup nearly to the top. Top each cup of batter with a large pinch of coconut, taking care to sprinkle it evenly over each cup.

5. Bake for 15 to 20 minutes.

6. Cool the muffins for at least 10 minutes before removing from the tin.

NUTRITIONAL FACTS (per 107-gram muffin)
Calories: 207 (12% from fat)

Fat: 3 g	Cholesterol: 20 mg	Carbohydrates: 44 g
Protein: 5 g	Fiber: 3.0 g	Sodium: 235 mg
Potassium: 372 mg	Iron: 1.6 mg	Calcium: 95 mg

Crunchy Granola Crumble Muffins

I have to admit that I got a bit caught up in my Crunchy Granola Crumble Muffins. Granola makes great-tasting muffins, but finding the best commercial brand—one that is low in fat and tastes great—took a lot of effort. Many granolas on the market are surprisingly high in fat and (can we talk?) don't taste very good. Before I was through searching, I guess I must have sampled every granola brand on the market, from those sold by major food companies to the chain-store brands to the bulk varieties sold in health food stores. I made muffins using each and every one.

You know what? No matter which brand I used, my muffins came out great every time, and they also had a lot of eye appeal. But when I conducted the nutritional analysis, I found that the fat content per muffin varied greatly. Wider still was the range of saturated fat in certain brands of granola. In the end, I chose General Mills Fruit Granola. While not the lowest in fat (Health Valley makes several varieties of fat-free granola), this brand has only 2.5 grams of fat per ⅔-cup serving, which makes little difference in the final fat-gram count. And, in my opinion, General Mills Fruit Granola brand is truly the most delicious.

Dry Ingredients	Wet Ingredients
1 cup whole-wheat flour	1¼ cups nonfat buttermilk
1 cup unbleached white flour	½ cup applesauce
2 teaspoons baking powder	½ cup maple syrup
½ teaspoon baking soda	2 large egg whites
½ teaspoon ground cinnamon	1 teaspoon vanilla extract
¼ teaspoon sea salt	1 teaspoon grated orange peel
1 cup low-fat granola	

CRUNCHY, CRUMBLY, SPICY DO-DA MUFFINS

Crumble Topping

½ cup low-fat granola

2 tablespoons whole-wheat flour

2 tablespoons unbleached white flour

⅛ teaspoon ground cinnamon

2 tablespoons light margarine, softened to room temperature

Yield: 12 muffins

1. Preheat the oven to 400° F.

2. To make the crumble topping, grind the granola in a food processor or hand-operated grinder until it resembles a coarse meal. Combine the granola, flours, and cinnamon in a bowl. Using a pastry blender or two knives, cut the margarine into this mixture to form a crumbly topping. Set aside.

3. Sift all of the dry ingredients, except the granola, together in a large bowl. Add the granola and stir to combine.

4. Whisk the wet ingredients in a medium bowl or blend them in a food processor. Pour the wet ingredients into the dry ingredients. Stir just until mixed. *Do not overstir.*

5. Spoon the batter into a greased or papered muffin tin. Fill each cup nearly to the top. Top each cup of batter with the crumble topping, taking care to spread it evenly over each cup. Too much topping piled high in the middle will prevent the muffins from rising properly.

6. Bake for 15 to 20 minutes.

7. Cool the muffins at least 10 minutes before removing from the tin.

NUTRITIONAL FACTS (per 86-gram muffin)
Calories: 181 (11% from fat)

Fat: 2 g	Cholesterol: 0 mg	Carbohydrates: 36 g
Protein: 5 g	Fiber: 2.5 g	Sodium: 236 mg
Potassium: 166 mg	Iron: 2.3 mg	Calcium: 108 mg

Double Ginger Ginger Muffins

Here's another installment in my crystallized-ginger series. These muffins are milder than my Gingerbread Muffins with Lemon Curd Filling (the ginger in these muffins will knock your socks off!). Unlike my Apple Ginger Muffins or Mango and Crystallized Ginger Muffins, in which the ginger takes a back seat to the main ingredients, these Double Ginger Ginger Muffins clearly intend to be gingery. Clocking in at less than 1 gram of fat per muffin, and deriving only 3 percent of their calories from fat, this is an excellent choice for a low-fat breakfast or snack.

Dry Ingredients	Wet Ingredients
1 cup whole-wheat flour	1 cup skim milk
1 cup unbleached white flour	½ cup water
½ cup brown rice flour	¼ cup honey
1½ teaspoons baking soda	¼ cup molasses
1 teaspoon baking powder	2 large egg whites
1 tablespoon ground ginger	1 tablespoon grated orange peel
¾ teaspoon ground cinnamon	
½ teaspoon ground nutmeg	
¼ teaspoon sea salt	

Goodies

½ cup golden raisins
3 tablespoons coarsely chopped crystallized ginger

Yield: 11–12 muffins

1. Preheat the oven to 400° F.

2. Sift the dry ingredients together in a large bowl.

3. Whisk the wet ingredients in a medium bowl or blend them in a food processor. Add the goodies and stir to combine.

4. Pour the wet mixture into the dry ingredients. Stir just until mixed. *Do not overstir.*

5. Spoon the batter into a greased or papered muffin tin. Fill each cup nearly to the top.

6. Bake for 15 to 20 minutes.

7. Cool the muffins at least 10 minutes before removing from the tin.

NUTRITIONAL FACTS (per 96-gram muffin)
Calories: 195 (3% calories from fat)

Fat: <1 g	Cholesterol: <1 mg	Carbohydrates: 45 g
Protein: 5 g	Fiber: 2.4 g	Sodium: 288 mg
Potassium: 275 mg	Iron: 1.9 mg	Calcium: 90 mg

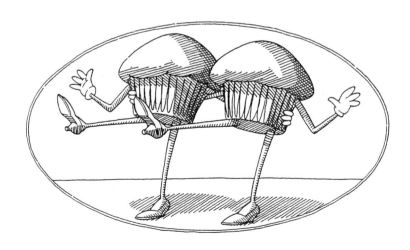

Girl Scout Date (and Nut) Muffins

When I was a Brownie, my troop leaders never failed to come up with fun and interesting things to make—to a kid, that is. We created papier-mâché clown puppets, glass-bead necklaces, leather wallets with laced plastic bindings—things a kid could easily make and appreciate. For me, the exception came during one meeting right before Christmas. The troop leaders arrived with baskets of whole dates, bowls of blanched almonds, and bags of finely grated coconut. They announced that we were going to make stuffed dates as Christmas presents for our parents.

I could relate to the almonds, but the coconut and dates were another matter. These were not food as I knew it. We were instructed to remove the pit from the dates, insert the almond where the pit had been, then roll the newly formed lump in the shredded coconut. We were assured that our parents would love them. Of course, I did as I was instructed, but I remember feeling bewildered during the entire project. I couldn't imagine that anyone was actually going to eat those things.

Time changes everything doesn't it? Now, I love them. And I created my Girl Scout Date (and Nut) Muffins to enjoy this flavor combination. With or without the almonds, they are great.

Dry Ingredients	Wet Ingredients
1¼ cups whole-wheat flour	1½ cups nonfat buttermilk
¾ cup unbleached white flour	¼ cup honey
1 teaspoon baking powder	¼ cup molasses
1 teaspoon baking soda	2 large egg whites
1½ teaspoons ground cinnamon	2 teaspoons grated orange peel
¼ teaspoon sea salt	1 teaspoon vanilla extract
2 tablespoons oat or wheat bran	

CRUNCHY, CRUMBLY, SPICY DO-DA MUFFINS

Goodies

¾ cup chopped dates
¼ cup flaked coconut

½ cup chopped roasted
almonds (optional)

Yield: 12 muffins

1. Preheat the oven to 400° F.

2. Sift all of the dry ingredients, except the oat or wheat bran, together in a large bowl. Add the bran and stir to combine. Add the goodies to the dry ingredients and toss to coat. (If the dates are particularly gooey, be sure to coat each bit well or they will clump together.)

3. Whisk the wet ingredients in a medium bowl or blend them in a food processor. Pour the wet ingredients into the dry mixture. Stir just until mixed. *Do not overstir.*

4. Spoon the batter into a greased or papered muffin tin. Fill each cup nearly to the top.

5. Bake for 15 to 20 minutes.

6. Cool the muffins at least 10 minutes before removing from the tin.

NUTRITIONAL FACTS (per 79-gram muffin without almonds)
Calories: 165 (5% from fat)

Fat: 1 g	Cholesterol: 0 mg	Carbohydrates: 37 g
Protein: 5 g	Fiber: 3.1 g	Sodium: 237 mg
Potassium: 240 mg	Iron: 1.7 mg	Calcium: 92 mg

NUTRITIONAL FACTS (per 84-gram muffin with almonds)
Calories: 199 (17% from fat)

Fat: 4 g	Cholesterol: 0 mg	Carbohydrates: 39 g
Protein: 6 g	Fiber: 3.7 g	Sodium: 238 mg
Potassium: 285 mg	Iron: 2.0 mg	Calcium: 109 mg

Jelly Crumb Muffins

Who doesn't like jelly-filled anything? I mean really. It's a marvelous invention. Firm sweet cake on the outside, moist and fruity center. Go for it.

What I especially like about these Jelly Crumb Muffins is that you can use any kind of jelly, jam, or fruit preserves. And you can use a number of different fillings in each batch. You can, for example, use your favorite jam in one or two muffins, your partner's favorite in another couple, your kid's in yet another two or three, and Aunt Tillie's favorite in what's left. You get the picture. It will seem as if you baked all day to get a variety of different muffins!

In my last batch, I used homemade blueberry-ginger preserves, which my friend Nancy bought while on an excursion through the backwoods of Maine. They were outrageous!

Dry Ingredients	Wet Ingredients
1 cup unbleached white flour	1 cup nonfat buttermilk
¾ cup whole-wheat flour	½ cup water
½ cup barley flour	½ cup honey
1 teaspoon baking powder	2 large egg whites
1 teaspoon baking soda	2 teaspoons grated lemon peel
¼ teaspoon sea salt	1 teaspoon vanilla extract

Goodies

⅜–½ cup all-fruit preserves

Crumble Topping

½ cup unbleached white flour

2 tablespoons light brown sugar

⅛ teaspoon ground cinnamon

2 tablespoons light margarine, softened to room temperature

CRUNCHY, CRUMBLY, SPICY DO-DA MUFFINS

Yield: 11–12 muffins

1. Preheat the oven to 400° F.

2. Prepare the crumble topping by combining the flour, brown sugar, and cinnamon in a medium bowl. Using a pastry blender or two knives, cut the margarine into this mixture to form a crumbly topping. Set aside.

3. Sift the dry ingredients together in a large bowl.

4. Whisk the wet ingredients in a medium bowl or blend them in a food processor. Pour the wet ingredients into the dry ingredients. Stir just until mixed. *Do not overstir.*

5. Spoon half the batter into greased or papered muffin cups. Place 1 teaspoon of the preserves on top of the batter in the center of each cup. Spoon the remaining batter into the cups, enclosing the preserves.

6. Top each cup of batter with the crumble topping, taking care to spread it evenly over each cup. Too much topping piled high in the middle will prevent the muffins from rising properly.

7. Bake for 15 to 20 minutes.

8. Cool the muffins for at least 10 minutes before removing from the tin.

NUTRITIONAL FACTS (per 99-gram muffin)
Calories: 220 (8% from fat)

Fat: 2 g	Cholesterol: <1 mg	Carbohydrates: 48 g
Protein: 5 g	Fiber: 2.6 g	Sodium: 233 mg
Potassium: 165 mg	Iron: 1.2 mg	Calcium: 63 mg

Prune Spice Muffins

When I first added the chopped prune bits to the dry ingredients in this recipe, I noticed that even after I tossed the bits around with my wooden spoon they remained clumped together.

"What am I going to do?" I thought. "The muffins will be globs of goo!"

"Get your hands into it," came a fun-loving inner voice.

Yeah. That's right. We don't have to be limited by manufactured tools, do we? Sometimes our hands are the best tools we have. Get your hands in it. Use your fingers to coat the individual prune bits with flour. It's a very satisfying experience.

To lower the fat content from 4 grams to less than 1 gram per muffin, simply eliminate the walnuts. And for a little added flavor, you might try making these muffins with Sunsweet Orange or Lemon-Essence Pitted Prunes. These add just the right hint of orange or lemon flavoring. My sister Barbara gave me that suggestion. It was a good one. Thanks, Barbie.

Dry Ingredients	Wet Ingredients
¾ cup whole-wheat flour	1 cup nonfat buttermilk
¾ cup unbleached white flour	¼ cup apple-juice concentrate
¾ cup barley flour	2 large egg whites
½ cup light brown sugar	
1½ teaspoons baking powder	
1 teaspoon baking soda	
1 teaspoon ground cinnamon	
1 teaspoon ground allspice	
½ teaspoon ground cloves	
¼ teaspoon sea salt	
2 tablespoons oat or wheat bran	

Goodies

¾ cup chopped prunes
½ cup chopped roasted walnuts (optional)

Yield: 11–12 muffins

1. Preheat the oven to 400° F.

2. Sift all of the dry ingredients, except the oat or wheat bran, together in a large bowl. Add the bran and stir to combine. Add the goodies and toss to coat (if necessary, use you hands to coat the gooey prune bits).

3. Whisk the wet ingredients in a medium bowl or blend them in a food processor. Pour the wet ingredients into the dry mixture. Stir just until mixed. *Do not overstir.*

4. Spoon the batter into a greased or papered muffin tin. Fill each cup nearly to the top.

5. Bake for 15 to 20 minutes.

6. Cool the muffins at least 10 minutes before removing from the tin.

NUTRITIONAL FACTS (per 77-gram muffin without walnuts)
Calories: 171 (2% from fat)

Fat: <1 g	Cholesterol: 0 mg	Carbohydrates: 39 g
Protein: 5 g	Fiber: 3.8 g	Sodium: 243 mg
Potassium: 255 mg	Iron: 1.5 mg	Calcium: 98 mg

NUTRITIONAL FACTS (per 82-gram muffin with walnuts)
Calories: 206 (11% from fat)

Fat: 4 g	Cholesterol: 0 mg	Carbohydrates: 40 g
Protein: 6 g	Fiber: 4.1 g	Sodium: 243 mg
Potassium: 283 mg	Iron: 1.6 mg	Calcium: 103 mg

Toasted Wheat Germ Crunch Muffins

I tend to forget that whole grain wheat is actually the seed of the wheat plant. The wheat seed is made up of three parts: the germ or embryo, the endosperms or food supply for the embryo, and the bran or protective coating for the seed.

Wheat germ is high in essential minerals and vitamins, especially vitamin E. It is also rich in calcium and magnesium and has been found to enhance the immune function. But it is also the most fragile part of the wheat seed. Its high oil content makes it vulnerable to decay. To protect the germ and delay spoilage, wheat germ is often toasted and stored in airtight containers. You will find toasted wheat germ in the cereal aisle of your grocery store.

I created my Toasted Wheat Germ Crunch Muffins to spotlight the nutty flavor and wholesome goodness of toasted wheat germ. If you like, try substituting ½ cup finely chopped roasted nuts for ½ cup of the wheat germ. This version will contain 202 calories, 4 grams of fat, no cholesterol, 35 grams of carbohydrates, 7 grams of protein, and 3.6 grams of fiber.

Dry Ingredients	Wet Ingredients
1¼ cups whole-wheat flour	1 cup nonfat buttermilk
1¼ cups unbleached white flour	½ cup water
1 tablespoon soy flour	¼ cup apple-juice concentrate
1½ teaspoons baking soda	¼ cup maple syrup
1 teaspoon baking powder	2 large egg whites
¼ teaspoon sea salt	1 teaspoon vanilla extract

Crunchy Topping	
1 cup honey crunch wheat germ	2 tablespoons light margarine,
½ cup light brown sugar	melted

Yield: 11–12 muffins

1. Preheat the oven to 400° F.

2. Sift the dry ingredients together in a large bowl.

3. Prepare the crunchy topping by combining the wheat germ and brown sugar in a medium bowl. Pour in the margarine and stir to combine. Retain ¾ cup of this mixture to top the muffins (see Step 5). Add the remaining mixture to the dry ingredients and stir to combine.

4. Whisk the wet ingredients in a medium bowl or blend them in a food processor. Pour the wet ingredients into the dry mixture. Stir just until mixed. *Do not overstir.*

5. Spoon the batter into a greased or papered muffin tin. Fill each cup nearly to the top. Generously top each cup of batter with the crunchy topping, taking care to spread it evenly over each cup. Too much topping piled in the middle will prevent the muffins from rising properly.

6. Bake for 15 to 20 minutes.

7. Cool the muffins at least 10 minutes before removing from the tin.

NUTRITIONAL FACTS (per 92-gram muffin)
Calories: 186 (6% from fat)

Fat: 1 g	Cholesterol: 0 mg	Carbohydrates: 37 g
Protein: 8 g	Fiber: 4.1 g	Sodium: 299 mg
Potassium: 308 mg	Iron: 1.9 mg	Calcium: 80 mg

Wheat Berry Muffins with Dates

Wheat is a fundamental food. It is grown on more acres than any other grain in the world. The wheat berry is the whole-grain wheat before it has been milled to make flour. You could say that all of my muffins contain wheat berries because they all contain whole-wheat or whole-wheat pastry flour. But this muffin spotlights the intact berry.

In this recipe, wheat berries are combined with dates—another food that has been consumed for centuries. When you bite into the hearty natural goodness of wheat berries and dates, get ready to join with millions of people who, through the ages, survived on these basic foods.

If you like wheat berries as much as I do, try adding them to your regular diet. Substituting boiled wheat berries for some of the rice in your favorite rice dish will add "chew appeal." With hot breakfast cereal, wheat berries add both flavor and nutrition. And boiled wheat berries are great all by themselves (sometimes I top them with a little apricot-mango chutney or a dab of shrimp paste).

Dry Ingredients	Wet Ingredients
1 cup whole-wheat pastry flour	1 cup skim milk
½ cup whole-wheat flour	½ cup applesauce
½ cup cornmeal	¼ cup apple butter
1 teaspoon baking powder	2 large egg whites
1 teaspoon baking soda	1 tablespoon molasses
¼ teaspoon sea salt	1 teaspoon grated lemon peel
¼ cup rolled oats	

Goodies	Topping
⅓ cup raw wheat berries	2 tablespoons dark brown sugar
¾ cup chopped dates	½ teaspoon ground cinnamon

CRUNCHY, CRUMBLY, SPICY DO-DA MUFFINS

Yield: 11–12 muffins

1. Place the wheat berries in 2 cups of water and bring to a boil over high heat. Reduce the heat to medium and cook the berries for 45 minutes. Drain and rinse with cold water. Set aside to cool.

2. Preheat the oven to 400° F.

3. Prepare the topping by combining the brown sugar and cinnamon in a small bowl. Set aside.

4. Sift all of the dry ingredients, except the rolled oats, together in a large bowl. Add the oats and stir to combine. Add the dates and the cooked wheat berries and toss to coat.

5. Whisk the wet ingredients in a medium bowl or blend them in a food processor. Pour the wet ingredients into the dry mixture. Stir just until mixed. *Do not overstir.*

6. Spoon the batter into a greased or papered muffin tin. Fill each cup nearly to the top. Top each cup of batter with the prepared topping, taking care to spread it evenly over each cup.

7. Bake for 15 to 20 minutes.

8. Cool the muffins at least 10 minutes before removing from the tin.

NUTRITIONAL FACTS (per 88-gram muffin)
Calories: 163 (3% from fat)

Fat: 1 g	Cholesterol: <1 mg	Carbohydrates: 37 g
Protein: 5 g	Fiber: 3.9 g	Sodium: 213 mg
Potassium: 296 mg	Iron: 1.3 mg	Calcium: 80 mg

4.

HERBY CHEESY MUFFIN THANGS

When most people think of muffins, they imagine sweet treats made with fruits and nuts and such. After all, muffins are usually relegated to the breakfast table. In my first book, *Gloria's Glorious Muffins*, I stretched muffins to their limits, devoting an entire chapter to a different kind of muffin—one that could be enjoyed with dinner and other meals. I left out the sweeteners and added veggies, cheeses, and herbs. These savory muffins are wonderful with soups, salads, casseroles, and just about every kind of meal imaginable. The "Herby Cheesy Muffin Thangs" found in this chapter follow that same vein. They include muffins made with a variety of herbs, cheeses, and vegetables. There's even a muffin made with beer.

My Lemon Cottage Dill Muffins go especially well with seafood dishes. The Ricotta Cheese with Basil and Rosemary Muffins and my Tomato Basil Muffins are perfect accompaniments to Italian-style meals. Serve refried beans with Modified Mexicali Corn Muffins. Soups and salads go hand-in-hand with Artichoke Hearts with Basil, Crumbled Bleu with Pear, French Onion, and Garden Vegetable Cream Cheese Muffins.

Artichoke Hearts with Basil Muffins

I was one happy camper when Kraft introduced a nonfat grated-cheese topping. "Okay," I told myself, "so it's not entirely freshly grated Parmesan (the olive of my Italian grandmother's eye), but it does contain some." And with 0 grams of fat per ounce compared to the 9 grams in regular Parmesan cheese, I owed it to myself to give it a try. Here's what I found.

There was no significant nutritional difference in the muffins that were made with freshly grated Parmesan and those made with the fat-free cheese product. The muffins contained the same number of calories, the fat and cholesterol content differed very little, and there was no appreciable difference in the sodium, potassium, iron, or calcium contents. I was surprised.

There are, however, two significant differences. First, the percentage of calories derived from fat per muffin is 22 percent with the real Parmesan cheese, and only 13 percent with the cheese product. That's important. Second, there is a significant difference in the flavor. The unmistakable Parmesan zing simply doesn't come through with the cheese product.

So, I'm leaving the choice to you. It's your call. If low-fat content is most important, choose the cheese product. But if it's flavor you're after and a bit more fat is not a concern, by all means, use the pure Parmesan.

Dry Ingredients	Wet Ingredients
1 cup whole-wheat pastry flour	1 cup vegetable broth, cooled to room temperature
½ cup unbleached white flour	¾ cup skim milk
¼ cup whole-wheat flour	1 tablespoon olive oil
2¼ teaspoons baking powder	2 large egg whites
¼ teaspoon sea salt	
¼ teaspoon ground black pepper	
½ cup grated Parmesan cheese or fat-free cheese topping	

Goodies

½ cup packed fresh basil (or ½ ounce), chopped
4 water-packed artichoke hearts, drained and chopped by hand
1 clove garlic, minced

Yield: 12 muffins

1. Preheat the oven to 400° F.

2. Sift all of the dry ingredients, except the cheese, together in a large bowl. Add the cheese and stir to combine.

3. Whisk the wet ingredients in a medium bowl or blend them in a food processor. Add the goodies and stir to combine.

4. Pour the wet mixture into the dry ingredients. Stir just until mixed. *Do not overstir.*

5. Spoon the batter into a greased or papered muffin tin. Fill each cup nearly to the top.

6. Bake for 15 to 20 minutes.

7. Cool the muffins at least 10 minutes before removing from the tin.

NUTRITIONAL FACTS (per 78-gram muffin with fat-free topping)
Calories: 91 (14% from fat)

Fat: 1 g	Cholesterol: <1 mg	Carbohydrates: 15 g
Protein: 5 g	Fiber: 2.7 g	Sodium: 290 mg
Potassium: 152 mg	Iron: 0.8 mg	Calcium: 131 mg

NUTRITIONAL FACTS (per 77-gram muffin with Parmesan cheese)
Calories: 92 (24% from fat)

Fat: 2 g	Cholesterol: 3 mg	Carbohydrates: 13 g
Protein: 5 g	Fiber: 1.7 g	Sodium: 287 mg
Potassium: 156 mg	Iron: 0.9 mg	Calcium: 137 mg

Cottage Cheese with Pear Muffins

For as long as I can remember, one of my mom's favorite lunchtime meals has been cottage cheese with sliced pears. She helped my sisters and I develop the habit of eating this light meal quite early in life. I never realized until recently what a low-fat (fat-free!) lunch it is. Since I love using cottage cheese in muffins—it makes them light and airy—and because pears are just as sweet and delicious as they can be, I decided to translate Mom's favorite lunch into this delectable muffin.

Because pears are so sweet and, when fully ripe, so soft, one might think that they would melt into oblivion as they bake. But the gritty nature of their flesh makes pears an ideal muffin ingredient. And it doesn't seem to matter if you use fresh pears or canned. Both hold their texture and flavor equally well.

Dry Ingredients	Wet Ingredients
1 cup whole-wheat flour	½ cup apple juice
1 cup unbleached white flour	½ cup skim milk
¼ cup light brown sugar	½ cup honey
1 teaspoon baking powder	2 large egg whites
1 teaspoon baking soda	1 tablespoon canola oil
½ teaspoon ground cardamom	
¼ teaspoon sea salt	

Goodies

1 cup nonfat cottage cheese
2 small pears, peeled and chopped (do not grate)

Yield: 11–12 muffins

1. Preheat the oven to 400° F.

2. Sift the dry ingredients together in a large bowl.

3. Whisk the wet ingredients in a medium bowl (do not use a food processor.) Add the goodies to the wet ingredients and stir to combine.

4. Pour the wet mixture into the dry ingredients. Stir just until mixed. *Do not overstir.*

5. Spoon the batter into a greased or papered muffin tin. Fill each cup nearly to the top.

6. Bake for 15 to 20 minutes.

7. Cool the muffins at least 10 minutes before removing from the tin.

NUTRITIONAL FACTS (per 108-gram muffin)
Calories: 153 (10% from fat)

Fat: 2 g	Cholesterol: 2 mg	Carbohydrates: 29 g
Protein: 6 g	Fiber: 2.4 g	Sodium: 275 mg
Potassium: 247 mg	Iron: 1.1 mg	Calcium: 68 mg

Crumbled Bleu with Pear Muffins

Whenever I visit my friend Nancy, who lives in Tennessee, we spend a fair amount of time reading about food in one or another of Nancy's four monthly food magazines. We share new dishes we have made since our last visit, or we just hang out in the kitchen while one or both of us prepares the next meal. It's a way of life with us. It's what we like to do.

The tantalizing aroma of lunch or dinner cooking often sets our stomachs to growling in anticipation of the meal to come and we want to eat before the meal is ready. One time, Nancy's husband, Will, and I were getting particularly hungry as Nancy put the final touches on the main course. She told us to get started on the appetizer. As Will and I eagerly took our seats, Nancy crossed the room and drew from the refrigerator a simple salad of sliced pears that were artistically arranged on a bed of red leaf lettuce and topped with a light sprinkling of crumbled bleu cheese. So simple—and yet so delicious that I wanted to skip the main course and eat another salad!

I think you will agree that the combination of bleu cheese and pear makes a marvelous muffin.

Dry Ingredients	Wet Ingredients
1¼ cups unbleached white flour	1 cup nonfat buttermilk
1 cup whole-wheat flour	1 cup water
½ cup brown rice flour	2 large egg whites
1½ teaspoons baking powder	2 tablespoons honey
1 teaspoon baking soda	
¼ teaspoon sea salt	

Goodies

½ cup crumbled bleu cheese
2 small pears, peeled and chopped (do not grate)

Yield: 12 muffins

1. Preheat the oven to 400° F.

2. Sift the dry ingredient together in a large bowl. Add the goodies and toss to coat.

3. Whisk the wet ingredients in a medium bowl or blend them in a food processor. Pour the wet ingredients into the dry mixture. Stir just until mixed. *Do not overstir.*

4. Spoon the batter into a greased or papered muffin tin. Fill each cup nearly to the top.

5. Bake for 15 to 20 minutes.

6. Cool the muffins at least 10 minutes before removing from the tin.

NUTRITIONAL FACTS (per 108-gram muffin)
Calories: 158 (12% from fat)

Fat: 2 g	Cholesterol: 3 mg	Carbohydrates: 30 g
Protein: 6 g	Fiber: 2.6 g	Sodium: 296 mg
Potassium: 161 mg	Iron: 1.2 mg	Calcium: 107 mg

French Onion Muffins

During the course of writing this cookbook, I discovered a number of new products that have made my task of creating delicious low-fat muffins easier. Alpine Lace Brands, Inc. of Maplewood, New Jersey, for example, makes a number of reduced-fat cheeses and cheese spreads that are perfect for muffins. Made with pasteurized skim milk, Alpine Lace cheeses have a low-fat content.

I use the reduced-fat Swiss cheese in these French Onion Muffins as well as the Oktoberfest Muffins on page 132. This cheese contains 25 percent less total fat and 53 percent less sodium than regular Swiss cheese. Yet it contains no artificial ingredients. And I like the effect it creates in my muffins. Like the Swiss cheese they contain, my muffins bake up with a lot of little holes where the chunks of Swiss have melted away.

Dry Ingredients	Wet Ingredients
1¼ cups whole-wheat flour	1 cup vegetable broth,
1 cup unbleached white flour	cooled to room temperature
1½ teaspoons baking powder	¾ cup skim milk
1 teaspoon baking soda	2 large egg whites
¼ teaspoon ground pepper	1 tablespoon soy sauce
½ cup nutritional yeast flakes	2 teaspoons Dijon mustard
	2 teaspoons honey

Goodies

3 tablespoons chopped onion
2 cloves garlic, minced
3 ounces Alpine Lace reduced-fat Swiss cheese, grated (or ¾ cup)
1½ tablespoons dried tarragon

Yield: 11–12 muffins

1. Preheat the oven to 400° F.

2. Sift all of the dry ingredients, except the yeast flakes, together in a large bowl.

3. In a small skillet over medium heat, toast the yeast flakes until they begin to brown. Add the toasted flakes to the dry ingredients and stir to combine.

4. Whisk the wet ingredients in a medium bowl or blend them in a food processor. Add the goodies and stir to combine.

5. Pour the wet mixture into the dry ingredients. Stir just until mixed. *Do not overstir.*

6. Spoon the batter into a greased or papered muffin tin. Fill each cup nearly to the top.

7. Bake for 15 to 20 minutes.

8. Cool the muffins at least 10 minutes before removing from the tin.

NUTRITIONAL FACTS (per 92-gram muffin)
Calories: 147 (14% from fat)

Fat: 2 g	Cholesterol: 6 mg	Carbohydrates: 24 g
Protein: 9 g	Fiber: 2.1 g	Sodium: 369 mg
Potassium: 257 mg	Iron: 2.3 mg	Calcium: 162 mg

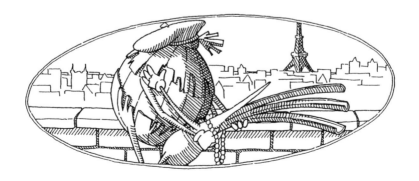

Garden Vegetable Cream Cheese Muffins

I've always enjoyed lightly seasoned muffins. They go with everything from salads and pasta dishes to casseroles and quiches. And they are great accompaniments for eggs at breakfast. So I was delighted when Kraft introduced their Philadelphia Brand Fat-Free Cream Cheese with Garden Vegetables. Almost simultaneously I became aware of Alpine Lace Fat-Free, Low-Cholesterol, Garden Vegetable cheese spread. Both products can be used successfully in this recipe.

For an added burst of flavor, try spreading a little additional cream cheese on these freshly baked muffins. And for another taste treat, try making these muffins with Kraft Fat-Free Cream Cheese with Pineapple. Add ½ cup coconut to the dry ingredients, delete the herbs and goodies, and skip Step 2. Enjoy your pineapple coconut muffins with Indian curry, Polynesian stir-fry dishes, or Chinese sweet-and-sour creations.

Dry Ingredients	Wet Ingredients
1½ cups whole-wheat flour	4 ounces fat-free cream cheese
1¼ cups unbleached white flour	with garden vegetables
2 tablespoons light brown sugar	2 cups water
1½ teaspoons baking powder	1 large egg
1½ teaspoons baking soda	1 teaspoon grated lemon rind
¼ teaspoon sea salt	
¼ cup oat bran	
½ teaspoon chopped basil	
½ teaspoon rubbed sage	
¼ teaspoon ground thyme	

Goodies

½ cup chopped onion

Yield: 12 muffins

1. Preheat the oven to 400° F.

2. Coat the bottom of a small skillet with nonstick cooking spray. Add the onion and sauté over medium heat until soft (about 5 minutes). Set aside to cool.

3. In a large bowl, sift together the following dry ingredients: the flours, brown sugar, baking powder, baking soda, and salt. Add the oat bran, basil, sage, and thyme, and stir to combine.

4. Using the purée blade of your food processor, cream the wet ingredients until they are well-blended. (You can also use a hand-held mixer at medium speed.) Add the cooled onion and stir to combine.

5. Pour the wet mixture into the dry ingredients. Stir just until mixed. *Do not overstir.*

6. Spoon the batter into a greased or papered muffin tin. Fill each cup nearly to the top.

7. Bake for 15 to 20 minutes

8. Cool the muffins at least 10 minutes before removing from the tin.

NUTRITIONAL FACTS (per 93-gram muffin)
Calories: 130 (7% from fat)

Fat: 1 g	Cholesterol: 19 mg	Carbohydrates: 19 g
Protein: 6 g	Fiber: 2.9 g	Sodium: 277 mg
Potassium: 184 mg	Iron: 1.6 mg	Calcium: 64 mg

Kasha Muffins with Browned Onion

We usually think of buckwheat as a breakfast food. This is probably because buckwheat flour is often used in pancakes and waffles, and porridge made with kasha (roasted buckwheat groats) is becoming an increasingly popular breakfast cereal in this country. However, kasha is a lot more versatile. It adds depth to stuffings and pilafs and can be served as a side dish instead of rice or potatoes. Another nice thing about kasha is that it takes very little time to cook, making it an ideal ingredient for muffins—quick and easy. I love kasha cooked with lots of onions—my inspiration for these fabulously hearty, unusual-tasting Kasha and Onion Muffins.

Many but not all grocery stores carry kasha. Look in the ethnic foods section or near the rice, grains, and beans. Some grocers stock it with the breakfast cereals. You may have to ask your grocer to special-order it for you. Popular brands include Near East and Wolff's.

Dry Ingredients	Wet Ingredients
1¼ cups unbleached white flour	1 cup vegetable broth,
¾ cup whole-wheat flour	cooled to room temperature
¼ cup soy flour	1 cup skim milk
1½ teaspoons baking powder	1 large egg
½ teaspoon baking soda	
¼ teaspoon sea salt	

Goodies

½ cup onion, chopped
¾ cup water
¼ cup kasha

Yield: 12 muffins

1. Preheat the oven to 400° F.

2. To prepare the goodies, coat the bottom of a small skillet with nonstick cooking spray. Add the onion and sauté over medium heat until soft (about 5 minutes). Reduce the heat and add the water and kasha. Simmer for 5 minutes. Remove from the heat and set aside to cool.

3. Sift the dry ingredients together in a large bowl.

4. Using the purée blade of your food processor, cream the wet ingredients until they are well-blended. (You can also use a hand-held mixer at medium speed.) Add the wet ingredients to the kasha-and-onion mixture. Stir to combine.

5. Pour the wet mixture into the dry ingredients. Stir just until mixed. *Do not overstir.*

6. Spoon the batter into a greased or papered muffin tin. Fill each cup nearly to the top.

7. Bake 15 to 20 minutes.

8. Cool the muffins at least 10 minutes before removing from the tin.

NUTRITIONAL FACTS (per 91-gram muffin)
Calories: 105 (11% from fat)

Fat: 1 g	Cholesterol: 18 mg	Carbohydrates: 20 g
Protein: 5 g	Fiber: 2.1 g	Sodium: 231 mg
Potassium: 173 mg	Iron: 1.2 mg	Calcium: 78 mg

Lemon Cottage Dill Muffins

I make two or three fish dishes that scream out for the perfect muffin. So I took one of my favorite recipes—Cosmic Cottage Dill Muffins—from my first book and revamped it. In this version, I have included fresh lemon peel and have replaced the dill seed with dill weed. Lemon brings out the flavor of whatever it accompanies. And dill weed has a subtle flavor that supports the flavor of fish. I proudly present Lemon Cottage Dill Muffins, the consummate muffin to enjoy with seafood.

You may be interested to learn that cottage cheese is not really cheese in the purest sense of the word because it is not cured. It is made with pasteurized skim milk to which lactic-acid cultures have been added. One of the reasons I like to use cottage cheese in muffins is that the melting curds of cheese create natural air pockets, giving the muffins a light texture. Small-curd cottage cheese works best because it creates perfect-sized pockets.

Dry Ingredients	Wet Ingredients
1¼ cups whole-wheat flour	1 cup nonfat cottage cheese
1 cup unbleached white flour	1 cup water
2 tablespoons sugar	½ cup skim milk
2½ teaspoons baking powder	2 large egg whites
¼ teaspoon sea salt	2½ tablespoons grated lemon peel

Goodies

3 tablespoons chopped fresh dill weed (or 1½ tablespoons dried)

Yield: 10 muffins

1. Preheat the oven to 400° F.

2. Sift the dry ingredients together in a large bowl. Add the dill weed and stir to combine.

3. Whisk the wet ingredients in a medium bowl (do not use a food processor). Pour the wet ingredients into the dry mixture. Stir just until mixed. *Do not overstir.*

4. Spoon the batter into a greased or papered muffin tin. Fill each cup nearly to the top.

5. Bake for 15 to 20 minutes.

6. Cool the muffins at least 10 minutes before removing from the tin.

NUTRITIONAL FACTS (per 96-gram muffin)
Calories: 126 (3% from fat)

Fat: <1 g	Cholesterol: 2 mg	Carbohydrates: 24 g
Protein: 7 g	Fiber: 2.3 g	Sodium: 229 mg
Potassium: 210 mg	Iron: 1.2 mg	Calcium: 102 mg

Modified Mexicali Corn Muffins

Until European explorers and conquerors returned home from the New World, their ships overflowing with new varieties of vegetation and wildlife, corn was grown only in the Americas. Historians agree that it grew wild in southern Mexico and Central America about 9,000 years ago and was finally cultivated by the Mayans some 6,000 years later. Corn played a key role in establishing the Mayan civilization.

Here's a real crowd-pleasing muffin—one that is excellent to serve at family get-togethers and potluck meals. It goes well with just about anything—egg dishes, tomato casseroles, Mexican bean dishes, even Indian curries. I call them Modified Mexicali Corn Muffins because I have taken the recipe from my first muffin cookbook and modified it to lower the fat content.

Dry Ingredients	Wet Ingredients
1½ cups yellow cornmeal	2 cups nonfat buttermilk
½ cup whole-wheat flour	1 tablespoon olive oil
½ cup unbleached white flour	1 large egg
1 tablespoon light brown sugar	
1½ teaspoons baking soda	
1 teaspoon baking powder	
¼ teaspoon sea salt	

Goodies

¼ cup chopped jalapeño peppers

¼ cup chopped pimentos

¾ cup frozen white or yellow corn, thawed and drained

Yield: 11–12 muffins

1. Preheat the oven to 400° F.

2. Sift the dry ingredients together in a large bowl.

3. Whisk the wet ingredients in a medium bowl or blend them in a food processor. Add the goodies and stir to combine.

4. Pour the wet mixture into the dry ingredients. Stir just until mixed. *Do not overstir.*

5. Spoon the batter into a greased or papered muffin tin. Fill each cup nearly to the top.

6. Bake for 15 to 20 minutes.

7. Cool the muffins at least 10 minutes before removing from the tin.

NUTRITIONAL FACTS (per 89-gram muffin)
Calories: 146 (15% from fat)

Fat: 2 g	Cholesterol: 19 mg	Carbohydrates: 27 g
Protein: 5 g	Fiber: 2.4 g	Sodium: 352 mg
Potassium: 146 mg	Iron: 1.2 mg	Calcium: 92 mg

Oktoberfest Muffins

When I lived in Virginia Beach, my friends and I loved to take day trips to Busch Gardens in Williamsburg. Sure, we liked the rides (I think I rode the Lock Ness Monster nine times one day), but the highlight of each trip was always the Bavarian pavilion. There we spent much of the day singing German beer-drinking songs and dancing the polka with people from all over the world. There was a fabulous feeling of camaraderie as we ate bratwurst on huge slices of rye bread and raised our beer steins to the ceiling in celebration of the harvest. Entranced by the excitement in the room, it was not difficult to imagine that we were attending a real harvest festival in Germany, a world away.

I tried to capture some of the flavor of that world in these Oktoberfest Muffins—the beer, the Swiss cheese, the unbeatable caraway and rye. I hope you enjoy them as much as I do.

Dry Ingredients	Wet Ingredients
1 cup unbleached white flour	1 cup flat beer at room
½ cup whole-wheat flour	temperature
½ cup barley flour	¾ cup skim milk
½ cup rye flour	2 tablespoons honey
2 tablespoons malt milk powder	1 tablespoon canola oil
1½ teaspoons baking powder	1 large egg
1 teaspoon baking soda	
¼ teaspoon sea salt	

Goodies

4 ounces Alpine Lace reduced-fat Swiss cheese, grated (or 1 cup)
2 teaspoons caraway seeds

Yield: 11–12 muffins

1. Preheat the oven to 400° F.

2. Sift the dry ingredients together in a large bowl.

3. Whisk the wet ingredients in a medium bowl or blend them in a food processor. Add the goodies and stir to combine.

4. Pour the wet mixture into the dry ingredients. Stir just until mixed. *Do not overstir.*

5. Spoon the batter into a greased or papered muffin tin. Fill each cup nearly to the top.

6. Bake for 15 to 20 minutes.

7. Cool the muffins at least 10 minutes before removing from the tin.

NUTRITIONAL FACTS (per 85-gram muffin)
Calories: 162 (15% from fat)

Fat: 3 g	Cholesterol: 26 mg	Carbohydrates: 27 g
Protein: 7 g	Fiber: 2.5 g	Sodium: 239 mg
Potassium: 160 mg	Iron: 1.2 mg	Calcium: 153 mg

When You Bake, Just Bake

I was watching the chickadees this morning as they visited the Audubon songbird feeder that Donna and Cashin gave me for my birthday. It's a fabulous feeder. The eighteen-or-so inch clear plastic tube has six portholes and the chickadees perch on small rods extending from each one. Two or three of them were taking turns poking their heads in the holes and wildly grabbing seed after seed. For every seed they managed to crack between their beaks, a dozen or more were cast about in the frenzy of the feed. (The scene bore a marked similarity to my own rummaging about in the sock drawer earlier this morning as I cast aside sock after sock in search of the mate to the one in my hand.) I watched the birds from my own perch just inside the sliding glass doors of my cottage on the edge of the woods. For the moment I was relaxed and calm, reflecting on the sight outside with a certain thoughtfulness.

The birds' frenzy reminded me of those days in the kitchen when I would get caught up with the hurry-up chatter inside my head, "Gotta get moving. Gotta hurry up and finish this batch of muffins so I can get to the next batch. Let's see. I've got two hours to bake four dozen muffins and clean up the kitchen. I've gotta work fast, fast, fast."

I would listen to the chatter as I zoomed around the kitchen at breakneck speeds finishing up one project so I could move on to the next. Mind you, nothing got done any faster than it would have if I was not hurrying. And the simply joy of baking escaped me entirely.

Baking is like meditating. It is most successful when we can muster some semblance of detachment from our inner world, when we are able to notice the chatter of the mind but not get caught up in it. Then when we bake, we just bake. For the moment, life is as it should be—simple and undisturbed, good enough as it is.

When we learn to relate to our inner world, as if from our own private cottage on the edge of the woods, we begin to notice that our mind is constantly running. And it doesn't matter which way. The point is that it is running. When we stop running with it, we are free to enjoy the simplicity of what we are doing.

When you bake, just bake. Let all of the chatter in your mind disappear into the magic of the moment.

Onion Corn Muffins

We have a delicacy in the South . . . Well, actually one would be hard-pressed to call it a delicacy. It's more like a regional specialty. I am speaking, of course, of hushpuppies. For those of you have never heard of them, hushpuppies are deep-fried balls of cornbread that are commonly enjoyed with pork barbecue or seafood. Everyone south of the Mason-Dixon line has a favorite restaurant and/or recipe for hushpuppies and it's not unusual to hear heated arguments over the best way to make them. In addition to the cornmeal, hushpuppies can be made with whole kernel corn, sautéed onions, or both. It's all according to taste.

It is these cornbread treats that inspired my Onion Corn Muffins. Try them with your favorite fish dinner or a big pot of pinto beans. Use your favorite cornmeal—white, yellow, or blue—and enjoy!

Dry Ingredients	Wet Ingredients
1¼ cups cornmeal	1¼ cups skim milk
¾ cup unbleached white flour	1 cup nonfat sour cream
½ cup whole-wheat flour	1 large egg
¼ cup sugar	
1½ teaspoons baking powder	
1 teaspoon baking soda	
¼ teaspoon sea salt	

Goodies

1 tablespoon light margarine
¼ cup finely chopped onion
1 cup frozen white or yellow corn, thawed and drained
¼ cup finely chopped fresh parsley

Yield: 12 muffins

1. Preheat the oven to 400° F.

2. Sift the dry ingredients together in a large bowl.

3. To prepare the goodies, melt the margarine in a skillet over medium heat. Add the onion and sauté until soft (about 5 minutes). Remove from the heat and add the corn and parsley. Stir to combine.

4. Whisk the wet ingredients in a medium bowl or blend them in a food processor. Add the goody mixture to the wet ingredients and stir to combine.

5. Pour the wet mixture into the dry ingredients. Stir just until mixed. *Do not overstir.*

6. Spoon the batter into a greased or papered muffin tin. Fill each cup nearly to the top.

7. Bake for 15 to 20 minutes.

8. Cool the muffins at least 10 minutes before removing from the tin.

NUTRITIONAL FACTS (per 100-gram muffin)
Calories: 158 (10% from fat)

Fat: 2 g	Cholesterol: 18 mg	Carbohydrates: 31 g
Protein: 6 g	Fiber: 2.2 g	Sodium: 243 mg
Potassium: 230 mg	Iron: 1.2 mg	Calcium: 108 mg

Pesto Muffins

If you are looking for a fabulous muffin to serve at a dinner party or to take to a potluck gathering, look no further. My Pesto Muffins are one of the most popular muffins I've created. I don't know anyone who doesn't like them. They go well with just about any cuisine, especially Italian.

However, I must warn you—when you take these muffins to a party, they will be such a hit that you might feel a little embarrassed at all the attention you'll get. Oh, and be sure to have copies of the recipe with you because everyone will ask you for it.

If you have my first cookbook, **Gloria's Glorious Muffins***, you may recognize these muffins, which I have revised to make lower in fat and higher in fiber than the original version.*

Dry Ingredients	Wet Ingredients
1 cup whole-wheat flour	1 cup vegetable broth, cooled to room temperature
½ cup whole-wheat pastry flour	1 cup nonfat buttermilk
½ cup unbleached white flour	½ cup water
2 teaspoons baking powder	2 large egg whites
¼ teaspoon sea salt	
½ cup grated Parmesan cheese or fat-free cheese topping	

Goodies

2 cloves garlic, minced

½ cup packed fresh basil (or ½ ounce), chopped

¼ cup chopped roasted walnuts

Yield: 10 muffins

1. Preheat the oven to 400° F.

2. Sift all of the dry ingredients, except the cheese, together in a large bowl. Add the cheese and stir to combine.

3. Whisk the wet ingredients in a medium bowl or blend them in a food processor. Add the goodies and stir to combine.

4. Pour the wet mixture into the dry ingredients. Stir just until mixed. *Do not overstir.*

5. Spoon the batter into a greased or papered muffin tin. Fill each cup nearly to the top.

6. Bake for 15 to 20 minutes.

7. Cool the muffins at least 10 minutes before removing from the tin.

NUTRITIONAL FACTS (per 98-gram muffin)
Calories: 134 (16% from fat)

Fat: 1 g	Cholesterol: 0 mg	Carbohydrates: 23 g
Protein: 7 g	Fiber: 3.4 g	Sodium: 484 mg
Potassium: 147 mg	Iron: 1.1 mg	Calcium: 127 mg

Potato Dill-Seed Muffins

When I tasted these muffins for the first time, I shrieked with glee, "That's just the combination of flavors I imagined, and it does taste wonderful!"

It is not uncommon for me to respond to food in such a way. Lest you think me immodest, perhaps I should explain that my enthusiasm for cooking comes from a relatively well-developed sense of taste. I can't help but get excited when that sense of taste meets a particularly fabulous combination of the earth's bounties. I can't contain myself. But, understand, I am not patting myself on the back for dreaming up this recipe, rather, I am applauding Mother Nature for creating the potatoes and the dill and the onion that become the muffin (how does She do that?).

Whether in potato salad, soup, or bread, the combination of potatoes and dill has always been one of my favorites. Try these muffins with broiled or grilled fish, especially salmon. Or enjoy them toasted with soft boiled eggs for breakfast. Mmm. Mmm.

Dry Ingredients	Wet Ingredients
1 cup whole-wheat pastry flour	¾ cup vegetable broth,
½ cup whole-wheat flour	cooled to room temperature
½ cup unbleached white flour	¾ cup skim milk
1½ teaspoons baking powder	½ cup nonfat cottage cheese
½ teaspoon baking soda	2 tablespoons honey
¼ teaspoon sea salt	1 tablespoon olive oil
1 cup instant potato flakes	1 large egg
(not powdered)	

Goodies

2 tablespoons chopped onion
2 tablespoons whole dill seeds

Yield: 10 muffins

1. Preheat the oven to 400° F.

2. Sift all of the dry ingredients, except the potato flakes, together in a large bowl. Add the potato flakes and stir to combine.

3. Whisk the wet ingredients in a medium bowl (do not use a food processor). Add the goodies and stir to combine.

4. Pour the wet mixture into the dry ingredients. Stir just until mixed. *Do not overstir.*

5. Spoon the batter into a greased or papered muffin tin. Fill each cup nearly to the top.

6. Bake for 15 to 20 minutes.

7. Cool the muffin at least 10 minutes before removing from the tin.

NUTRITIONAL FACTS (per 87-gram muffin)
Calories: 140 (16% from fat)

Fat: 2 g	Cholesterol: 23 mg	Carbohydrates: 25 g
Protein: 6 g	Fiber: 2.4 g	Sodium: 293 mg
Potassium: 241 mg	Iron: 1.2 mg	Calcium: 111 mg

Ricotta Cheese with Basil and Rosemary Muffins

Ricotta cheese is a wonderful source of protein. It contains about 18 grams per half-cup serving. It is also very high in phosphorus, essential amino acids, and calcium (a whopping 660 milligrams per half-cup). And it has nearly twice the recommended daily allowance of vitamin A. None of these reasons, however, is why my brother-in-law Bob is often seen holding the refrigerator door open with his right hip, carton of ricotta cheese in right hand, tablespoon in left, and cheeks bulging as he savors this late-night snack. My niece Laura says she can hear him mmm-ing with Italian delight from two rooms away.

That's how it is with ricotta-cheese lovers. And there's only one thing that can make the pleasure even greater—a touch of fresh basil and rosemary. Whether or not you are a ricotta-cheese lover, I think you will find these muffins hard to resist. So don't. Make them right away!

Dry Ingredients	Wet Ingredients
1 cup whole-wheat flour	1 cup low-fat ricotta cheese
1 cup unbleached white flour	1 cup vegetable broth,
½ cup rye flour	cooled to room temperature
1½ teaspoons baking powder	¾ cup skim milk
1 teaspoon baking soda	1 tablespoon olive oil
¼ teaspoon sea salt	1 large egg

Goodies

4 teaspoons chopped fresh basil (or 2 teaspoons dried)
1 teaspoon chopped fresh rosemary (or ½ teaspoon dried)

Yield: 11–12 muffins

1. Preheat the oven to 400° F.

2. Sift the dry ingredients together in a large bowl. Add the goodies and stir to combine.

3. Whisk the wet ingredients in a medium bowl (do not use a food processor). Pour the wet ingredients into the dry mixture. Stir just until mixed. *Do not overstir.*

4. Spoon the batter into a greased or papered muffin tin. Fill each cup nearly to the top.

5. Bake for 15 to 20 minutes.

6. Cool the muffins at least 10 minutes before removing from the tin.

NUTRITIONAL FACTS (per 94-gram muffin)
Calories: 138 (20% from fat)

Fat: 3 g	Cholesterol: 25 mg	Carbohydrates: 22 g
Protein: 6 g	Fiber: 2.3 g	Sodium: 326 mg
Potassium: 142 mg	Iron: 1.1 mg	Calcium: 112 mg

Roasted Red Pepper Muffins

My sister Betty gave me a jar of roasted red peppers for Christmas last year along with a basketful of interesting sauces and condiments. Right away, of course, I thought about making a roasted red pepper muffin. But I waited. I deliberated. I didn't so much as sift the flour until I got a sign from heaven indicating the perfect ingredients to go along with it. I think roasted red pepper deserves this kind of deliberation, don't you?

One afternoon, as I was searching through the cheese department at my local grocery store, I saw it. Tucked away on the far right of the refrigerated display, next to the strawberry Neufchatel and the goat's milk cheese was a six-ounce container of fat-free cream cheese with garlic and herbs by Alpine Lace. "Eureka." I knew instantly it was the sign I had been waiting for.

In addition to tasting great—light and flavorfully rich—this brand of cream cheese contains no fat, less than 5 milligrams of cholesterol, and only 30 calories per one-ounce serving (regular cream cheese contains 100 calories).

Dry Ingredients	Wet Ingredients
1 cup whole-wheat flour	6 ounces Alpine Lace garlic and
1 cup unbleached white flour	herb cream cheese, softened
½ cup brown rice flour	1¼ cups skim milk
1½ teaspoons baking powder	1 tablespoon olive oil
1 teaspoon baking soda	1 large egg
¼ teaspoon sea salt	

Goodies

2 teaspoons chopped fresh rosemary (or 1 teaspoon dried)
½ cup chopped roasted red peppers

Yield: 11–12 muffins

1. Preheat the oven to 400° F.

2. Sift the dry ingredients together in a large bowl.

3. Using the purée blade of your food processor, cream the wet ingredients until they are well blended. (You can also use a hand-held mixer at medium speed.) Add the goodies and stir to combine.

4. Pour the wet mixture into the dry ingredients. Stir just until mixed. *Do not overstir.*

5. Spoon the batter into a greased or papered muffin tin. Fill each cup nearly to the top.

6. Bake for 15 to 20 minutes.

7. Cool the muffins at least 10 minutes before removing from the tin.

NUTRITIONAL FACTS (per 85-gram muffin)
Calories: 147 (14% from fat)

Fat: 2 g	Cholesterol: 23 mg	Carbohydrates: 24 g
Protein: 7 g	Fiber: 1.8 g	Sodium: 311 mg
Potassium: 195 mg	Iron: 1.2 mg	Calcium: 135 mg

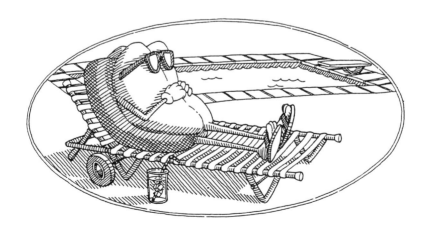

Scarborough Fair Muffins

Last Christmas, Nancy and Will gave me three pottery herb jars that were handcrafted by their friend Margie. The jars contained sage, rosemary, and thyme, which Nancy had grown in her garden and dried in late fall. To help me identify the herbs within, Margie had taken a sprig of each herb and pressed them into the still-wet clay. This created a fossil-like impression of each herb on the baked jars. Beautiful. As much decoration as culinary necessity, my new jars of herbs assumed an honored position on the shelf above the stove.

A few weeks later, I was in the kitchen baking the morning away when I realized I had been singing "Scarborough Fair" as I worked. I glanced over to the shelf above the stove and recognized immediately what had triggered my song—sage, rosemary, and thyme. Well, one thought led to another and there was Paul Simon in my mind's eye. I smiled as I recalled the many, many hours of sheer delight he has given me through his music. "I should write and thank him for being the poet laureate of my life," I thought.

I never did write to Paul Simon. Instead I thanked him with my Scarborough Fair Muffins. He writes songs, I create muffins. It's all a celebration of life.

Dry Ingredients	Wet Ingredients
1½ cups whole-wheat pastry flour	1 cup vegetable broth,
½ cup whole-wheat flour	cooled to room temperature
½ cup unbleached white flour	½ cup nonfat buttermilk
½ cup rye flour	½ cup water
2 teaspoons baking powder	2 tablespoons honey
1 teaspoon baking soda	1 tablespoon olive oil
¼ teaspoon sea salt	1 large egg
	1 teaspoon grated lemon peel

Goodies

1 tablespoon chopped fresh parsley (or 1½ teaspoons dried)
1½ teaspoons chopped fresh sage (or ¾ teaspoon dried)
1½ teaspoons chopped fresh rosemary (or ¾ teaspoon dried)
1½ teaspoons chopped fresh thyme (or ¾ teaspoon dried)

Yield: 11 muffins

1. Preheat the oven to 400° F.

2. Sift the dry ingredients together in a large bowl. Add the goodies and stir to combine.

3. Whisk the wet ingredients in a medium bowl or blend them in a food processor. Pour the wet ingredients into the dry mixture. Stir just until mixed. *Do not overstir.*

4. Spoon the batter into a greased or papered muffin tin. Fill each cup nearly to the top.

5. Bake for 15 to 20 minutes.

6. Cool the muffins at least 10 minutes before removing from the tin.

NUTRITIONAL FACTS (per 82-gram muffin)
Calories: 132 (15% from fat)

Fat: 2 g	Cholesterol: 19 mg	Carbohydrates: 25 g
Protein: 5 g	Fiber: 2.6 g	Sodium: 327 mg
Potassium: 132 mg	Iron: 1.4 mg	Calcium: 93 mg

Sun-Dried Tomato Corn Muffins with Cumin

Randy and Steven always seem to find fabulous breads to serve with their delicious light dinners of fresh salad, sliced cheese, and fruit. One evening they served a sun-dried tomato bread from a local bakery that was out of sight. Its reddish color suggested that it was made with tomato juice. And it contained just enough cumin seeds to set things off. We sat there, as we often do, with our eyes closed savoring the flavors, commenting on what we liked, and determining what we might do differently if we baked the bread. "Corn," I said. "It wants corn." Thus my recipe for Sun-Dried Tomato Corn Muffins with Cumin was born.

To cut down on fat, I use plain sun-dried tomatoes (not those packed in oil). If you choose to use the oil-packed variety, you can skip the hydrating instruction in Step 1.

Dry Ingredients	Wet Ingredients
1 cup unbleached white flour	1 cup tomato juice
1 cup yellow or white cornmeal	1 cup nonfat buttermilk
½ cup whole-wheat flour	1 tablespoon olive oil
2 teaspoons baking soda	1 tablespoon honey
½ teaspoon baking powder	1 large egg
¼ teaspoon sea salt	
¼ teaspoon ground black pepper	

Goodies
½ cup sun-dried tomatoes
1 teaspoon cumin seeds

Yield: 11–12 muffins

1. Soak the sun-dried tomatoes in ½ cup of boiling water for about 15 minutes. Drain and discard the water. Chop the hydrated tomatoes into pea-sized bits. Add the cumin seeds and stir to combine. Set aside.

2. Preheat the oven to 400° F.

3. Sift the dry ingredients together in a large bowl.

4. Whisk the wet ingredients in a medium bowl or blend them in a food processor. Add the goody mixture from Step 1 and stir to combine.

5. Pour the wet mixture into the dry ingredients. Stir just until mixed. *Do not overstir.*

6. Spoon the batter into a greased or papered muffin tin. Fill each cup nearly to the top.

7. Bake for 15 to 20 minutes.

8. Cool the muffins at least 10 minutes before removing from the tin.

NUTRITIONAL FACTS (per 89-gram muffin)
Calories: 137 (16% from fat)

Fat: 2 g	Cholesterol: 19 mg	Carbohydrates: 26 g
Protein: 5 g	Fiber: 2.2 g	Sodium: 371 mg
Potassium: 245 mg	Iron: 1.6 mg	Calcium: 55 mg

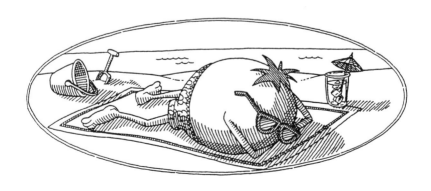

Tomato Basil Muffins

According to the American Spice Trade Association, the amount of basil sold between 1981 and 1991 rose 187 percent. I would estimate that during the same period, my own use of this herb increased by about 1000 percent! Gone are the days when I used basil only for tomato sauce and garlic bread. Even then I used only a pinch in an entire pot of tomato sauce or a dash or two on the garlic bread. Now I find I throw half the bottle in the pot. Or better yet, I drive over to Diana and Nancy's, whose backyard overflows with some thirty-odd basil plants in four or five varieties. Because they have a hard time maintaining these plants, they encourage me to "top" them every few weeks. Thank goodness. I fill a large picnic basket each time I go. This makes it possible for me to saturate my muffins with fresh sweet basil.

Don't be shy with the basil in these muffins. You won't regret it. Pack as many leaves as you can fit into a half-cup, then either chop them by hand or let your food processor do the work. Between the basil and the sun-dried tomatoes, these muffins are bursting with flavor. They are a great compliment to any pasta dish or salad.

Dry Ingredients	Wet Ingredients
1½ cups whole-wheat flour	¾ cup water
½ cup whole-wheat pastry flour	2 tablespoons tomato sauce
½ cup unbleached white flour	1 tablespoon olive oil
1½ teaspoons baking soda	1 tablespoon honey
½ teaspoon baking powder	1 large egg
¼ teaspoon sea salt	
¼ teaspoon ground black pepper	

Goodies

½ cup sun-dried tomatoes
½ cup packed fresh basil (or ½ ounce), chopped
1 clove garlic, minced

Yield: 10 muffins

1. Soak the sun-dried tomatoes in ½ cup of boiling water for about 15 minutes. Drain and discard the water. Chop the hydrated tomatoes into pea-sized bits. Add the basil and garlic and stir to combine. Set aside.

2. Preheat the oven to 400° F.

3. Sift the dry ingredients together in a large bowl.

4. Whisk the wet ingredients in a medium bowl or blend them in a food processor. Add the goody mixture from Step 1 and stir to combine.

5. Pour the wet mixture into the dry ingredients. Stir just until mixed. *Do not overstir.*

6. Spoon the batter into a greased or papered muffin tin. Fill each cup nearly to the top.

7. Bake for 15 to 20 minutes.

8. Cool the muffins at least 10 minutes before removing from the tin.

NUTRITIONAL FACTS (per 81-gram muffin)
Calories: 131 (17% from fat)

Fat: 2 g	Cholesterol: 21 mg	Carbohydrates: 24 g
Protein: 5 g	Fiber: 3.2 g	Sodium: 330 mg
Potassium: 257 mg	Iron: 1.6 mg	Calcium: 37 mg

5.

CHOCOLATE EVERY-WHICH-WAY-BUT-FAT MUFFINS

The first time I looked at the USDA Food Guide Pyramid (see page 29), I let out a quiet chuckle. I immediately imagined a chocolate cake and a hot fudge sundae sitting there at the peak. "Yup," I thought. "That's where I'd put chocolate—right on the capstone of the pyramid, the part closest to heaven. Seriously, though. That uppermost part of the pyramid includes foods that, while pleasing to the taste, are high in calories and fat and low in nutrition. It is recommended that no more than 30 percent of one's daily calories be derived from them.

When you first examine chocolate, the news is not good. Pound for pound, chocolate contains twelve times the calories found in yogurt or cooked carrots, six times the calories found in fresh bananas, and nearly four times the calories found in boneless/skinless chicken breast. And chocolate derives close to half of those calories from fat. But the good news is that chocolate can be combined with other, more nutritious ingredients to produce foods that are likewise nutritious—and delicious.

So I devoted an entire chapter to muffins made with chocolate. With the exception of Chocolate Raspberry Chambord Muffins, none of the muffins in this chapter contains more than 250 calories. And none derives more than 15 percent of its calories from fat. All are made with wholesome, nutritious ingredients. There is a muffin for every kind of chocolate—chocolate mint, milk chocolate, semi-sweet chocolate, and even white chocolate.

Of the available cocoa powders, I have found Hershey's European-Style Cocoa Powder—unsweetened chocolate with most of the cocoa butter or fat removed—to be the darkest and richest. But feel free to use whatever brand you like best. For a special treat, try using gourmet cocoa powders, which are sold in specialty shops. Just be aware that they may contain more fat than most commercial brands.

Banana (Nut) Fudge Muffins

Enjoying the simple pleasures of life isn't always easy. Take hot fudge banana splits, for example. Whenever I try to enjoy one, self-denigrating thoughts often get in the way.

"Oh, you're bad!"

"Where's your self control?"

"Why don't you just smear it on your thighs?"

I don't know where these thoughts come from. They just appear out of nowhere to torment me. Then I have to say, "Quiet down, you silly thoughts. I'm simply trying to pay attention to the taste buds dancing inside my mouth." Sometimes it works, sometimes it doesn't. And when I can't control the thoughts, they almost always interfere with the pleasure of the moment.

I created Banana (Nut) Fudge Muffins to mirror the flavors I enjoy so much in hot fudge banana splits. When I first bit into one of these muffins, I didn't hear the critical voices. Do you think the chatterbox inside our heads is controlled by a fat meter?

Dry Ingredients	Wet Ingredients
1 cup whole-wheat flour	3 ripe bananas, mashed
¾ cup unbleached white flour	(or 1½ cups)
½ cup barley flour	¾ cup skim milk
¾ cup light brown sugar	½ cup coffee, cooled to
1½ teaspoons baking powder	room temperature
1 teaspoon baking soda	2 large egg whites
¼ teaspoon sea salt	2 teaspoons vanilla extract

Goodies	Nut Topping (optional)
⅓ cup coarsely chopped	1 egg white
milk chocolate	½ cup coarsely chopped
	roasted walnuts

Yield: 12 muffins

1. Preheat the oven to 400° F.

2. Sift the dry ingredients together in a large bowl. Add the chocolate to the dry ingredients and stir to combine.

3. Whisk the wet ingredients in a medium bowl or blend them in a food processor. Pour the wet ingredients into the dry mixture. Stir just until mixed. *Do not overstir.*

4. Spoon the batter into a greased or papered muffin tin. Fill each cup nearly to the top.

5. Prepare the topping (if using). Whip the egg white until it forms soft peaks, then add the walnuts and stir to coat completely. Top each cup of batter with a heaping teaspoon of the topping, taking care to spread it evenly over each cup. Too much topping piled in the middle will prevent the muffins from rising properly.

6. Bake for 15 to 20 minutes.

7. Cool the muffins at least 10 minutes before removing from the tin.

NUTRITIONAL FACTS (per 103-gram muffin without walnut topping)
Calories: 193 (10% from fat)

Fat: 2 g	Cholesterol: 2 mg	Carbohydrates: 40 g
Protein: 5 g	Fiber: 2.7 g	Sodium: 276 mg
Potassium: 242 mg	Iron: 0.9 mg	Calcium: 77 mg

NUTRITIONAL FACTS (per 105-gram muffin with walnut topping)
Calories: 209 (16% from fat)

Fat: 4 g	Cholesterol: 2 mg	Carbohydrates: 40 g
Protein: 5 g	Fiber: 2.8 g	Sodium: 276 mg
Potassium: 255 mg	Iron: 1.0 mg	Calcium: 79 mg

Chocolate Almond Muffins

One of the things I miss most about living in the Northeast—besides being able to visit my Aunts Mary, Annie, Helen, and Marie, and my Uncle John and Aunt Dot anytime I want—is the abundance of fantastic Italian grocery stores and restaurants. I miss the parmigiana, lasagne, scaloppine, cacciatora, calzones, and cannoli, made as only a true paisano knows how. And the biscotti. I miss the biscotti.

Imagine my delight when I went into my favorite frozen-yogurt bar one afternoon and discovered that the owners had expanded their product line to include not only quality Italian coffees—espresso, cappuccino—in a variety of flavors, but also a first-rate biscotti. As I stood there reading the menu posted high above polished copper and brass coffee machines, my eyes were drawn to a large glass cookie jar situated above the open freezers of Italian ice. Could it be? Chocolate almond biscotti? I completely forgot the frozen yogurt that brought me into the store as I sat down to enjoy chocolate almond biscotti dunked in a fresh cup of cappuccino. It was this that inspired my Chocolate Almond Muffins.

There are many kinds of almonds ranging from sweet to quite bitter. If you had almond trees in your yard, you would be able to tell by the color of their spring blossoms which trees produce bitter almonds and which produce sweet ones. Trees with pink blossoms bear sweet almonds—the ones we eat. White-blossomed trees produce bitter nuts, which are used to make extracts.

Dry Ingredients	Wet Ingredients
1½ cups whole-wheat flour	1¼ cups skim milk
1¼ cups unbleached white flour	½ cup applesauce
½ cup light brown sugar	½ cup honey
6 tablespoons cocoa powder	2 large egg whites
1½ teaspoons baking soda	2 teaspoons almond extract
1 teaspoon baking powder	1 teaspoon vanilla extract
¼ teaspoon sea salt	

Goodies	Topping
¼ cup coarsely chopped milk chocolate	⅓ cup sliced almonds

Yield: 12 muffins

1. Preheat the oven to 400° F.

2. Sift the dry ingredients together in a large bowl. Add the chocolate and stir to combine.

3. Whisk the wet ingredients in a medium bowl or blend them in a food processor. Pour the wet ingredients into the dry mixture. Stir just until mixed. *Do not overstir.*

4. Spoon the batter into a greased or papered muffin tin. Fill each cup nearly to the top. Top each muffin with a large pinch of sliced almonds, taking care to sprinkle them evenly over each cup.

5. Bake for 15 to 20 minutes.

6. Cool the muffins at least 10 minutes before removing from the tin.

NUTRITIONAL FACTS (per 101-gram muffin)
Calories: 233 (13% from fat)

Fat: 3 g	Cholesterol: 2 mg	Carbohydrates: 46 g
Protein: 6 g	Fiber: 3.3 g	Sodium: 299 mg
Potassium: 329 mg	Iron: 2.1 mg	Calcium: 84 mg

Chocolate Cherry Muffins

When my friend Randy asked me how the cookbook was going, I told him I was facing one of the biggest challenges of my life—finding a way to make chocolate muffins that are rich and moist but low in fat! "Any ideas?" I asked him.

Turns out that Randy was the right person to ask. He is one of the few people I know who truly understands the seriousness of these matters. He works in a fabulous bookstore in Durham, North Carolina, called The Regulator, where he has distinguished himself as someone who always knows what's happening in the publishing world—be it literature, travel, fashion, food, or whatever. "Have you tried making your chocolate muffins with prunes?" he asked. He told me that more and more bakers are using prunes as a substitute for the usual fat— butter, margarine, oil—in baked goods. He said he had used prunes in a brownie recipe and claimed they were among the best he had ever eaten.

I did some experimentin' and discovered that Randy was right. Prunes are just what I had been looking for. They are, oh, so sweet. And with almost no fat, zero cholesterol, tons of fiber, and very little sodium, prunes are, quite literally, just what the doctor ordered. They even look like chocolate! Well, sort of. Using prunes in these Chocolate Cherry Muffins makes it possible to create a sweet and delicious chocolate muffin with only one gram of fat. Way to go, Randy.

Dry Ingredients	Wet Ingredients
1¼ cups whole-wheat flour	1½ cups skim milk
¾ cup unbleached white flour	2 large egg whites
½ cup whole-wheat pastry flour	2 teaspoons vanilla extract
¾ cup sugar	2 teaspoons cherry flavoring
½ cup cocoa powder	
1½ teaspoons baking powder	
1 teaspoon baking soda	
¼ teaspoon sea salt	

Prune Purée	Goodies
¼ cup pitted prunes	½ cup dark sweet cherries,
¼ cup skim milk	pitted and chopped

Yield: 12 muffins

1. Preheat the oven to 400° F.

2. Sift the dry ingredients together in a large bowl. Add the cherries and toss to coat.

3. Purée the prunes and milk in a food processor or blender to produce a smooth paste. Add the wet ingredients and pulse to combine.

4. Pour the wet mixture into the dry mixture. Stir just until mixed. *Do not overstir.*

5. Spoon the batter into a greased or papered muffin tin. Fill each cup nearly to the top.

6. Bake for 15 to 20 minutes.

7. Cool the muffins at least 10 minutes before removing from the tin.

NUTRITIONAL FACTS (per 91-gram muffin)
Calories: 166 (5% from fat)

Fat: 1 g	Cholesterol: 1 mg	Carbohydrates: 35 g
Protein: 6 g	Fiber: 3.4 g	Sodium: 161 mg
Potassium: 395 mg	Iron: 2.2 mg	Calcium: 101 mg

Chocolate Chestnut Muffins

When I was a kid growing up in Dunellen, New Jersey, we had a chestnut tree on the east side of our house. My sisters and I used it as home base when we played hide and seek. "Ollie, Ollie, Oxen Free." And it was a great climbing tree until the lowest limb grew too high for us to reach. In the fall, the ground was covered with chestnuts encased in thorny green spheres. With such an obtrusive casing, I wonder how Mother Nature expected anyone to liberate the feast inside! To tell you the truth, I don't think we ever did. I mean I don't remember actually eating chestnuts. I think we just let the squirrels carry them away for the winter.

Chestnuts contain less than 1 gram of fat per ounce and derive only 8 percent of their calories from fat. This is very unusual for a nut. Most nuts derive far more than the recommended 30 percent of their calories from fat (see Crazy About Nuts and Seeds beginning on page 82). My favorite nuts, walnuts, contain 18 grams of fat per ounce and derive 87 percent of their calories from fat! And macadamia nuts contain a whopping 21 grams of fat per ounce and derive 95 percent of their calories from fat.

Needless to say, with my interest in eating lower-fat foods, I've reacquainted myself with chestnuts. These Chocolate Chestnut Muffins are a way for you to do the same.

Dry Ingredients	Wet Ingredients
1 cup whole-wheat flour	1¼ cups skim milk
¾ cup unbleached white flour	½ cup nonfat sour cream
½ cup whole-wheat pastry flour	¼ cup honey
¾ cup sugar	2 large egg whites
6 tablespoons cocoa powder	2 teaspoons vanilla extract
1½ teaspoons baking soda	
1 teaspoon baking powder	
¼ teaspoon sea salt	

Goodies

1 cup coarsely chopped roasted chestnuts
⅓ cup coarsely chopped milk chocolate

Yield: 12–13 muffins

1. Preheat the oven to 400° F.

2. Sift the dry ingredients together in a large bowl. Reserve ½ cup of the chestnuts to top the muffins (see Step 4). Add the remaining chestnuts and the chocolate to the dry ingredients and stir to combine.

3. Whisk the wet ingredients in a medium bowl or blend them in a food processor. Pour the wet ingredients into the dry mixture. Stir just until mixed. *Do not overstir.*

4. Spoon the batter into a greased or papered muffin tin. Fill each cup nearly to the top. Top each cup of batter with about 2 heaping teaspoons of roasted chestnuts, taking care to spread them evenly over each cup.

5. Bake for 15 to 20 minutes.

6. Cool the muffins at least 10 minutes before removing from the tin.

NUTRITIONAL FACTS (per 88-gram muffin)
Calories: 193 (11% from fat)

Fat: 2 g	Cholesterol: 2 mg	Carbohydrates: 38 g
Protein: 6 g	Fiber: 3.5 g	Sodium: 303 mg
Potassium: 341 mg	Iron: 1.7 mg	Calcium: 85 mg

Chocolate-Chip Banana Muffins

If I didn't include a low-fat chocolate-chip banana muffin in this book, I think the chocolate and banana lovers of the world would have my head. It's a great combination, isn't it? I couldn't imagine leaving this recipe out.

For an added treat with this and any of the muffins that call for chopped chocolate, try substituting a rich (and expensive!) specialty chocolate for the commercial baking chips. True, you will be adding a bit more fat, but the added fat will be divided between a dozen or so muffins.

Dry Ingredients	Wet Ingredients
1½ cups unbleached white flour	3 ripe bananas, mashed
1 cup whole-wheat flour	(or 1½ cups)
½ cup light brown sugar	¾ cup skim milk
1½ teaspoons baking soda	2 large egg whites
1 teaspoon baking powder	2 teaspoons vanilla extract
¼ teaspoon sea salt	

Goodies

½ cup mini semi-sweet chocolate chips

Yield: 11–12 muffins

1. Preheat the oven to 400° F.

2. Sift the dry ingredients together in a large bowl. Add the chocolate chips and stir to combine.

3. Whisk the wet ingredients in a medium bowl or blend them in a food processor. Pour the wet ingredients into the dry mixture. Stir just until mixed. *Do not overstir.*

4. Spoon the batter into a greased or papered muffin tin. Fill each cup nearly to the top.

5. Bake for 15 to 20 minutes.

6. Cool the muffins at least 10 minutes before removing from the tin.

NUTRITIONAL FACTS (per 93-gram muffin)
Calories: 203 (14% from fat)

Fat: 3 g	Cholesterol: <1 mg	Carbohydrates: 40 g
Protein: 5 g	Fiber: 2.8 g	Sodium: 238 mg
Potassium: 234 mg	Iron: 1.8 mg	Calcium: 53 mg

Chocolate Ginger Muffins

When I returned from my first three-month retreat at an English monastery, I brought back several boxes of chocolate-covered ginger. You know how it is when you go to a foreign country for the first time. You are excited to return with a slice of its uniqueness to delight and please family and friends. Columbus brought back corn, Magellan, spices. I returned with chocolate ginger.

My enthusiasm, however, was crushed by the response. It seemed that no one was particular interested in my chocolate ginger—except Mom, who is connected to everything English by means of sympathetic resonance with her United Kingdom ancestry. "How can you not like it?" I asked the others. "This candy is so fabulous! I don't get it." I ended up eating most of it myself.

However, I'm not one to give up easily. When it came time to dream up muffins for my new cookbook, I included Chocolate Ginger Muffins. The smooth dark chocolate warms my palate like a satin down comforter and the sting of crystallized ginger really gets my attention and connects me with the here and now. The response from others? My friend Gwen's daughter Megan said, "Mom and I liked the chocolate part just fine, but that ginger kept getting in the way."

What can I say? I guess it is an acquired taste. Is there anyone else out there who finds this a fabulous combination?

Dry Ingredients	Wet Ingredients
1 ¼ cups unbleached white flour	1 cup nonfat buttermilk
½ cup whole-wheat pastry flour	¾ cup water
½ cup whole-wheat flour	1 tablespoon canola oil
½ cup brown rice flour	2 large egg whites
½ cup sugar	½ cup honey
6 tablespoons cocoa powder	1½ teaspoons vanilla extract
1½ teaspoons baking soda	
1 teaspoon baking powder	
¼ teaspoon sea salt	

Goodies

¼ cup coarsely chopped crystallized ginger

Yield: 11–12 muffins

1. Preheat the oven to 400° F.

2. Sift the dry ingredients together in a large bowl. Add the ginger and toss to coat.

3. Whisk the wet ingredients in a medium bowl or blend them in a food processor. Pour the wet ingredients into the dry mixture. Stir just until mixed. *Do not overstir.*

4. Spoon the batter into a greased or papered muffin tin. Fill each cup nearly to the top.

5. Bake for 15 to 20 minutes.

6. Cool the muffins at least 10 minutes before removing from the tin.

NUTRITIONAL FACTS (per 96-gram muffin)
Calories: 215 (8% from fat)

Fat: 2 g	Cholesterol: 0 mg	Carbohydrates: 46 g
Protein: 5 g	Fiber: 2.3 g	Sodium: 260 mg
Potassium: 254 mg	Iron: 1.9 mg	Calcium: 68 mg

Chocolate Mint Muffins

Preparing to bake my first batch of these Chocolate Mint Muffins found me headed out the back door towards the huge patch of mint that grows between the gladiolas and gloriosa daisies on the south side of my deck. When I arrived there, however, I was disappointed to find only two stalks left. "Hmm," I thought, "I guess I've been putting too much mint in my daily pitchers of iced tea. My use must have exceeded the plant's ability to reproduce itself!" I harvested what I could and was happy to discover that the plant still contained the 30 to 40 leaves I needed to make the 2½ tablespoons of chopped mint.

These muffins are light—both in texture and flavor. They are great as is, but as an added treat, try frosting them with Nonfat Cream-Cheese Icing (page 174) or Yogurt-Cheese Icing (see inset beginning on page 168) and serving them with sliced strawberries. Mmm. Mmm. Mmm. And if you don't mind adding another three or four fat grams per muffin, include ¼ cup coarsely ground semi-sweet chocolate-mint chips to this recipe.

Dry Ingredients	Wet Ingredients
1 cup whole-wheat pastry flour	1½ cups skim milk
1 cup unbleached white flour	2 large egg whites
½ cup whole-wheat flour	2 teaspoons vanilla extract
½ cup sugar	
6 tablespoons cocoa powder	
1½ teaspoons baking powder	
1 teaspoon baking soda	
¼ teaspoon sea salt	

Prune Purée	Goodies
½ cup pitted prunes	2½ tablespoons chopped fresh
¼ cup skim milk	mint (or 1 tablespoon dried)

Yield: 12 muffins

1. Preheat the oven to 400° F.

2. Sift the dry ingredients together in a large bowl. Add the mint and stir to combine.

3. Purée the prunes and milk in a food processor or blender to produce a smooth paste. Add the wet ingredients and pulse to combine.

4. Pour the wet mixture into the dry mixture. Stir just until mixed. *Do not overstir.*

5. Spoon the batter into a greased or papered muffin tin. Fill each cup nearly to the top.

6. Bake for 15 to 20 minutes.

7. Cool the muffins at least 10 minutes before removing from the tin.

NUTRITIONAL FACTS (per 82-gram muffin)
Calories: 147 (4% from fat)

Fat: 1 g	Cholesterol: 1 mg	Carbohydrates: 31 g
Protein: 5 g	Fiber: 2.7 g	Sodium: 213 mg
Potassium: 245 mg	Iron: 1.9 mg	Calcium: 100 mg

Making Yogurt-Cheese Icing

When it came time to frost my muffins, I found myself facing a real dilemma. After successfully creating delicious muffins that are very nearly fat-free, I wasn't about to ruin them with the usual high-fat icings that are made with butter, margarine, or cream cheese. Always ready for a challenge, I created a luscious nonfat icing made with yogurt cheese.

CHOOSING THE RIGHT YOGURT

To make yogurt-cheese icing, first choose the best ingredients—the best yogurt. The following tips are provided to help you when making your selection:

■ Start with good, clean yogurt.

What I mean is, select a product that is made from natural ingredients. Many yogurts on the market today contain large amounts of fat, artificial sweeteners, and artificial flavors. And some so-called yogurts aren't yogurt at all but a conglomeration of ingredients (including milk solids and gelatin) that are added to milk to create a custardy consistency.

■ Select yogurt that suits your dietary needs.

The United States Food and Drug Administration (FDA) recognizes three standardized yogurt products:

• Yogurt that is made from whole milk and has at least 3.25 percent milk from fat.

• Low-fat yogurt that is made from low-fat milk or part-skim milk and has between 2 and 0.5 percent milk fat.

• Nonfat yogurt that is made from skim milk and contains less than 0.5 percent milk fat.

Depending on the fat content you prefer, you can make yogurt cheese with any one of these products. (*See* Table 5.1 Nutrient Analysis of Yogurt Varieties, on page 171.)

I've done taste tests with each of these yogurt types. When it comes to eating yogurt right from the container, I like the product made from low-fat milk best. It is 98 percent fat-free and tastes richer and creamier than the nonfat variety. However, when making yogurt-cheese icing, I use plain nonfat yogurt because I am most interested in making an icing that contains no fat at all. Besides, even when made with non-fat yogurt, the icing is rich, creamy, and sweet.

■ Select yogurt that contains active cultures.

All yogurt is made with active cultures. That's what makes it yogurt. Once made, however, some yogurt is heated for longer shelf life. This heating process kills all the active yogurt cultures—the "good" bacteria that you want to eat. Before selecting a yogurt, be sure the label says, "active yogurt cultures," "living yogurt cultures," or "contains active cultures." If the product has been heat treated, the FDA requires that this information must be stated on the label.

STEPS IN MAKING YOGURT-CHEESE ICING

You have made an educated choice in selecting the best yogurt for your icing. Now it is time to make the yogurt cheese.

Make the Yogurt Cheese

Yogurt cheese is made by draining fresh yogurt through a fine cloth or sieve until the whey separates from the solids. (Some people add a little lemon juice to facilitate this process.)

To make about a cup of yogurt cheese, follow these simple steps:

1. Line a strainer with cheesecloth or a large coffee filter. Place the strainer over a suitable bowl.

2. Spoon 2 cups of yogurt into the lined strainer and cover with a plate or plastic wrap. Place in the refrigerator to drain.

3. For yogurt cheese with the consistency of sour cream, drain the yogurt for 4 to 6 hours.

For yogurt cheese with the consistency of whipped cream cheese, drain the yogurt for 12 hours. And for yogurt cheese with the consistency of cream cheese (the best for making icing), allow the yogurt to drain for 24 hours or longer.

Instead of draining the yogurt through a strainer, you can use a filter-lined cone of an automatic drip coffee maker. Or you can use a specially designed yogurt-cheese funnel, which is sold at most kitchen shops, specialty food stores, and health food stores.

Make the Yogurt-Cheese Icing

Yogurt-cheese icing is a bit more fragile than icing made with butter or cream cheese. If you beat it hard with an electric mixer it will become soupy. Hand mixing is best. And for the best results, be sure to use well-drained yogurt cheese that has the consistency of cream cheese.

To make basic Nonfat Yogurt-Cheese Icing, do the following:

1. In a medium bowl, add 1 cup of sifted powdered sugar and 1 teaspoon of vanilla to 1 cup of yogurt cheese. Stir to the desired consistency.

2. Cover and refrigerate until ready to use.

3. Use to frost muffins that have been cooled to room temp.

And don't be afraid to experiment! You can make yogurt-cheese icing with any flavored yogurt. (Just be sure to avoid those that contain gelatin—they won't separate properly.) For example, for my Marvelous Marbled Muffins with Coffee Yogurt-Cheese Icing (page 178), first I make yogurt cheese from coffee-flavored yogurt, then I add sifted powdered sugar to make the icing.

Good luck and have fun experimenting with these delicious nonfat frostings.

Table 5.1   Nutrient Analysis of Yogurt Varieties

The nutritional breakdown of the following yogurt varieties is based on 8-ounce (1 cup) servings.

Yogurt Type	Calories	Fat gms	Chol. mgs	Protein gms	Calcium mgs
Nonfat	140	<1	5	14	499
Low-Fat	159	4	15	13	458
Whole Milk	150	8	31	8	295

Chocolate Raspberry Chambord Muffins

A few years back, when I was still knee-deep in the corporate world, my room-mate received a distinctive Christmas gift—a chocolate bourbon cake. It was like no cake I had ever tasted. Soaked in bourbon, wrapped in light plastic, and stored in a round decorative tin, the cake was so rich that we could eat only a thin slice at a time. And it was so moist that it was more like an English pudding than cake. Because of the liquor, the cake lasted for what seemed like forever.

That was the first time I tasted cake that had been preserved with liquor. Since then I've enjoyed a number of similar cakes—and made a few myself. It occurred to me that I could soak muffins with liquors or liqueurs. Why not? Such muffins would grace any holiday table or simply be the perfect topper for an elegant dinner. These Chocolate Raspberry Chambord Muffins are the first in my collection. (Other recipes that call for liquor include Blueberry Peach-Schnapps Muffins on page 194, and Grand Marnier Creamsicle Muffins on page 208). Try them topped with a dollop of low-fat whipped-cream topping.

Dry Ingredients	Wet Ingredients
1¼ cups whole-wheat flour	1 cup buttermilk
1¼ cups unbleached white flour	½ cup water
½ cup sugar	½ cup honey
6 tablespoons cocoa powder	2 large egg whites
1½ teaspoons baking soda	2 teaspoon raspberry flavoring
1 teaspoon baking powder	1 teaspoon vanilla extract
¼ teaspoon sea salt	

Goodies

¾ cup firm fresh raspberries* (about 6 ounces), washed, patted dry, and halved

½ cup coarsely chopped semi-sweet chocolate

* Can use frozen raspberries that have been thawed, drained, and patted dry.

Glaze

¼ cup Chambord (or other raspberry liqueur)

Yield: 12 muffins

1. Preheat the oven to 400° F.

2. Sift the dry ingredients together in a large bowl. Add the goodies and toss to coat.

3. Whisk the wet ingredients in a medium bowl or blend them in a food processor. Pour the wet ingredients into the dry mixture and stir just until mixed, taking care not to break the raspberries. *Do not overstir.*

4. Spoon the batter into a greased or papered muffin tin. Fill each cup nearly to the top.

5. Bake for 15 to 20 minutes.

6. Remove the muffins from the oven. Using a skewer or toothpick, immediately pierce the top of each muffin in six or seven places. Drizzle the liqueur over each muffin until all of it is absorbed. Leave the muffins in the tin at least 20 minutes before removing.

NUTRITIONAL FACTS (per 100-gram muffin)
Calories: 267 (11% from fat)

Fat: 3 g	Cholesterol: 0 mg	Carbohydrates: 54 g
Protein: 6 g	Fiber: 3.8 g	Sodium: 257 mg
Potassium: 266 mg	Iron: 2.7 mg	Calcium: 65 mg

Devil's Food Muffins with Nonfat Cream-Cheese Icing

The way I see it, chocolate is one of life's essentials. There's food, clothing, shelter, and chocolate. Right? Then why haven't we treated chocolate with the proper respect? I mean, how is it that we've come to associate chocolate cake, for example, with sin and guilt and overindulgence, while white cake is food for angels? I think names such as death-by-chocolate and devil's food have placed chocolate in the wrong light and have conditioned us to feel wicked when we needn't.

Here's a muffin that will change any of your negative associations with chocolate. As you bite into one of these iced delights, bear in mind that it contains only one gram of fat and derives only four percent of its calories from fat. So you needn't feel devilish, unless, of course, you want to.

Dry Ingredients	Wet Ingredients
1½ cups unbleached white flour	1½ cups nonfat buttermilk
¾ cup whole-wheat flour	½ cup chocolate syrup
¾ cup sugar	2 large egg whites
6 tablespoons cocoa powder	1½ teaspoons vanilla extract
1 teaspoon baking powder	
1 teaspoon baking soda	
¼ teaspoon sea salt	

Nonfat Cream-Cheese Icing

4 ounces nonfat cream cheese
1 cup powdered sugar, sifted
1 teaspoon vanilla extract

Yield: 12 muffins

1. Preheat the oven to 400° F.

2. Sift the dry ingredients together in a large bowl.

3. Whisk the wet ingredients in a medium bowl or blend them in a food processor. Pour the wet ingredients into the dry ingredients. Stir just until mixed. *Do not overstir.*

4. Spoon the batter into a greased or papered muffin tin. Fill each cup nearly to the top.

5. Bake for 15 to 20 minutes.

6. While the muffins bake, prepare the icing. Using a hand-held mixer or blender, cream together the cream cheese, powdered sugar, and vanilla extract to an icing consistency. Do not use a food processor. Cover and refrigerate until ready to frost the muffins.

7. Cool the muffins at least 10 minutes before removing from the tin. Allow them to cool to room temperature before frosting.

NUTRITIONAL FACTS (per 99-gram muffin)
Calories: 224 (4% from fat)

Fat: 1 g	Cholesterol: 2 mg	Carbohydrates: 48 g
Protein: 7 g	Fiber: 2.2 g	Sodium: 277 mg
Potassium: 262 mg	Iron: 1.9 mg	Calcium: 99 mg

Double Chocolate Chocolate Muffins

Half of all women say they'd choose chocolate over sex any day. At least that's what Debra Waterhouse writes in her book **Why Women Need Chocolate**. *Waterhouse explains that women's preference for chocolate may be due to the fact that it is about half sugar, which raises serotonin or blood sugar levels, producing an exhilarating (although temporary) "high." Chocolate also includes fat, which boosts endorphins—those natural little opiates manufactured by the brain; phenylethylamine, which behaves much like the neurological chemical that is released when we fall in love; and caffeine, which gives a nice little boost both physically and mentally.*

No wonder women like it.

I guess the moral of the story is twofold: If you're a woman, skip the sex and try my Double Chocolate Chocolate Muffins. If you're a man who loves a woman, don't bake her my Double Chocolate Chocolate Muffins.

You might be surprised (as I was) to learn that chocolate contains much less caffeine than coffee and most soft drinks. There are 20 milligrams of caffeine in a one-ounce serving of dark chocolate. A six-ounce cup of coffee contains 100 milligrams and a twelve-ounce soft drink contains 35 to 50. I was also surprised to learn that milk chocolate contains even less caffeine than the dark variety— only 6 milligrams per one-ounce serving.

Dry Ingredients	Wet Ingredients
1¼ cups whole-wheat flour	1¾ cups nonfat buttermilk
1 cup unbleached white flour	½ cup honey
½ cup sugar	1 large egg
6 tablespoons cocoa powder	1½ teaspoons vanilla extract
1¼ teaspoons baking soda	
1 teaspoon baking powder	
¼ teaspoon sea salt	

Goodies

⅓ cup coarsely chopped milk chocolate

Yield: 12 muffins

1. Preheat the oven to 400° F.

2. Sift the dry ingredients together in a large bowl. Add the chocolate and stir to combine.

3. Whisk the wet ingredients in a medium bowl or blend them in a food processor. Pour the wet ingredients into the dry mixture. Stir just until mixed. *Do not overstir.*

4. Spoon the batter into a greased or papered muffin tin. Fill each cup nearly to the top.

5. Bake for 15 to 20 minutes.

6. Cool the muffins at least 10 minutes before removing from the tin.

NUTRITIONAL FACTS (per 88-gram muffin)
Calories: 213 (12% from fat)

Fat: 3 g	Cholesterol: 19 mg	Carbohydrates: 43 g
Protein: 6 g	Fiber: 2.5 g	Sodium: 314 mg
Potassium: 244 mg	Iron: 1.9 mg	Calcium: 92 mg

Marvelous Marbled Muffins with Coffee Yogurt-Cheese Icing

One night, Gwen and I met at Penny Universitie Coffeehouse & Deli, a fun café just up Main Street from the North Carolina School of the Arts. We wanted to grab a bite before going to see an Arthur Miller play presented by the school's third-year drama students. I had just torn off a piece of my fresh-baked German pretzel and Gwen was about to take a sip of her decaf cappuccino when the waiter delivered Gwen's sandwich to our table. We both said "ah" at the same time. It was just a simple turkey and Havarti sandwich with lettuce and tomato, but its marbleized rye and pumpernickel bread made it distinctive.

Marbled anything tends to have that effect—very impressive. That's why I wanted to include a marbled muffin in this cookbook. And I was so happy with both the appearance and flavor of these Marvelous Marbled Muffins that I decided to top them with coffee-flavored yogurt-cheese icing and serve them as a low-fat dessert. I chose coffee yogurt because I love the combination of coffee and chocolate. However, you can make any flavored yogurt-cheese icing. May I suggest vanilla or banana? (See Making Yogurt-Cheese Icing beginning on page 168.) Or, if you'd like, skip the icing and serve these muffins sliced and topped with a scoop of nonfat black cherry frozen yogurt.

Dry Ingredients	Wet Ingredients
1¼ cups whole-wheat flour	1½ cups nonfat buttermilk
1¼ cups unbleached white flour	½ cup water
¾ cup sugar	2 large egg whites
1½ teaspoons baking soda	3 teaspoons vanilla extract
1 teaspoon baking powder	
¼ teaspoon sea salt	

Coffee Yogurt-Cheese Icing	Goodies

1 cup powdered sugar
½ cup coffee-flavored yogurt cheese
  (*see* page 171)
	¼ cup coarsely chopped
	  semi-sweet chocolate
	3 tablespoons cocoa powder

Yield: 12 muffins

1. Preheat the oven to 400° F.

2. Sift the dry ingredients together in a large bowl. Divide the dry ingredients in half and place in two bowls. Add the goodies to one bowl and stir to combine.

3. Whisk the wet ingredients in a medium bowl or blend them in a food processor. Pour half of the wet ingredients into each bowl of dry ingredients. Stir just until mixed. *Do not overstir.*

4. In a greased or papered muffin tin, spoon a scant quarter cup of the chocolate batter in each cup. Top with a scant quarter cup of the vanilla batter. Divide any remaining batter evenly among the cups. With a knife, gently swirl the batters in each cup to create a marble-like effect.

5. Bake for 15 to 20 minutes.

6. While the muffins bake, prepare the icing. Sift the powdered sugar in a small bowl. Add the yogurt cheese. Using a spoon, stir the mixture to an icing consistency. Do not use a food processor, blender, or electric mixer. Cover and refrigerate the icing until ready to frost the muffins.

7. Cool the muffins at least 10 minutes before removing from the tin. Allow them to cool to room temperature before frosting.

NUTRITIONAL FACTS (per 102-gram muffin)
Calories: 187 (10% from fat)

Fat: 2 g	Cholesterol: 1 mg	Carbohydrates: 37 g
Protein: 6 g	Fiber: 2.5 g	Sodium: 280 mg
Potassium: 214 mg	Iron: 1.8 mg	Calcium: 102 mg

Orange Chocolate Muffins

Susan just called to compliment me on the muffins I brought her this morning on my way to the health food store. I had delivered them just as she, her husband, George, and her son, Douglas, were about to sit down to a (as Susan put it) not-too-interesting lunch. "We were so excited about having muffins with our meal," said Susan, "that before we sat down, I cleared the kitchen counters of their clutter, loaded the dishwasher, and set the table with my favorite tablecloth and dishes."

The thought of the three of them enjoying the muffins in this way made me happy. That's exactly why I love to bake muffins and give them away. They always seem to turn ordinary events into something special.

"But that's not all I want to tell you." Susan said, and she went on to explain that the three of them agreed to each select a different muffin, take a bite, then pass the muffin around the table for the others to taste as well. However, when George took the first bite of his Orange Chocolate Muffin, he playfully refused to pass it around the table! He wanted to keep it all to himself.

These muffins were inspired by the orange-flavored reception sticks that my friends Steven and Randy always offer after their fabulous dinner parties. These thin sticks of hard candy have been hand-dipped in dark chocolate and are usually served with after-dinner coffee.

Dry Ingredients	Wet Ingredients
1¼ cups whole-wheat flour	1¼ cups skim milk
1¼ cups unbleached white flour	½ cup honey
¼ cup sugar	¼ cup orange-juice concentrate
1½ teaspoons baking soda	2 large egg whites
1 teaspoon baking powder	3 tablespoons grated orange peel
¼ teaspoon sea salt	1½ teaspoons vanilla extract

Goodies

½ cup coarsely chopped semi-sweet chocolate

Yield: 12 muffins

1. Preheat the oven to 375° F.

2. Sift the dry ingredients together in a large bowl. Add the chocolate and stir to combine.

3. Whisk the wet ingredients in a medium bowl or blend them in a food processor. Pour the wet ingredients into the dry mixture. Stir just until mixed. *Do not overstir.*

4. Spoon the batter into a greased or papered muffin tin. Fill each cup nearly to the top.

5. Bake for 15 to 20 minutes.

6. Cool the muffins at least 10 minutes before removing from the tin.

NUTRITIONAL FACTS (per 88-gram muffin)
Calories: 202 (14% from fat)

Fat: 3 g	Cholesterol: <1 mg	Carbohydrates: 40 g
Protein: 5 g	Fiber: 2.7 g	Sodium: 281 mg
Potassium: 197 mg	Iron: 1.8 mg	Calcium: 55 mg

Pumpkin Chocolate-Chip Muffins

It seems like I am always looking for new and interesting ways to prepare pumpkin. I have found these to be great muffins to serve for the holidays.

I use canned pumpkin purée in this recipe—mostly because it is always available and easy to use. You can, of course, make your own pumpkin purée. Start with a firm pumpkin that is without soft spots. (One pound of raw pumpkin will yield about one cup cooked purée.) Cut the pumpkin into quarters and scrape away the seeds and stringy stuff. Then cut the quarters into smaller pieces. Cook these pieces in a six- or eight-quart pot of boiling water until tender (about 20 minutes). Drain and cool the pumpkin before peeling away the outer skin. Mash the pumpkin by hand or purée it in a food processor. Add water as needed.

Dry Ingredients	Wet Ingredients
1½ cups unbleached white flour	1 cup pumpkin purée
1 cup whole-wheat flour	1 cup skim milk
¾ cup light brown sugar	2 large egg whites
1½ teaspoons baking powder	1 teaspoon vanilla extract
1 teaspoon baking soda	
1½ teaspoons ground cinnamon	
½ teaspoon ground nutmeg	
½ teaspoon ground allspice	
¼ teaspoon ground cloves	
¼ teaspoon sea salt	

Goodies

⅓ cup mini semi-sweet chocolate chips
⅓ cup chopped roasted walnuts (optional)

Yield: 12 muffins

1. Preheat the oven to 400° F.

2. Sift the dry ingredients together in a large bowl. Add the goodies and stir to combine.

3. Whisk the wet ingredients in a medium bowl or blend them in a food processor. Pour the wet ingredients into the dry mixture. Stir just until mixed. *Do not overstir.*

4. Spoon the batter into a greased or papered muffin tin. Fill each cup nearly to the top.

5. Bake for 15 to 20 minutes.

6. Cool the muffins at least 10 minutes before removing from the tin.

NUTRITIONAL FACTS (per 92-gram muffin without walnuts)
Calories: 190 (11% from fat)

Fat: 2 g	Cholesterol: <1 mg	Carbohydrates: 39 g
Protein: 5 g	Fiber: 2.9 g	Sodium: 210 mg
Potassium: 223 mg	Iron: 2.2 mg	Calcium: 93 mg

NUTRITIONAL FACTS (per 96-gram muffin with walnuts)
Calories: 211 (18% from fat)

Fat: 4 g	Cholesterol: <1 mg	Carbohydrates: 40 g
Protein: 5 g	Fiber: 3.0 g	Sodium: 210 mg
Potassium: 240 mg	Iron: 2.3 mg	Calcium: < 96 mg

Roger's Chocolate Fruit-and-Nut Muffins

Last year, on the Sunday before Christmas, my nephew Roger had just returned from an overnight trip to Philadelphia with his sister Annie and cousin Laura. Roger is a minister of a congregational church and the girls had made the turn-around trip with him to hear him preach. Before leaving on Saturday, I had packed them a bag of assorted muffins for the trip. Roger returned from the trip, hungry and tired and asking for more muffins.

"You're in luck," I told him. "There was a special on bananas yesterday at Laneco's, and I just baked some Coco Nana, Better Banana (Nut) Bran, and Orange Strawberry Banana muffins. Which would you like?"

"Aunt Gloria," he said, "I . . . er . . . um . . . a . . . I'm kind of allergic to bananas. I mean, I get a stomachache when I eat them." I could see he was choosing his words carefully so as not to hurt my feelings. Roger is considerate like that. Always has been. "Have you got any other kind?"

Well, I didn't have any other muffins on hand, but that only gave me an excuse to whip up a batch of something special. I asked Roger what would please him. "Well," he said, "I just tasted a Cadbury chocolate bar with fruit and nuts and loved it."

These are for you, Roger. I was going to name them Roger's Anything But Banana Muffins—but you get the point. I hope I am never again without a muffin you can enjoy.

Dry Ingredients	Wet Ingredients
1 cup whole-wheat flour	1¼ cups skim milk
1 cup unbleached white flour	½ cup nonfat sour cream
2 teaspoons baking powder	¼ cup chocolate syrup
½ cup light brown sugar	2 large egg whites
6 tablespoons cocoa powder	1 tablespoon canola oil
¼ teaspoon sea salt	2 teaspoons vanilla extract
	1 teaspoon grated orange peel

Goodies

½ cup raisins

⅓ cup chopped roasted walnuts

Yield: 12 muffins

1. Preheat the oven to 400° F.

2. Sift the dry ingredients together in a large bowl.

3. Whisk the wet ingredients in a medium bowl or blend them in a food processor. Add the goodies to the wet ingredients and stir to combine.

4. Pour the wet mixture into the dry ingredients. Stir just until mixed. *Do not overstir.*

5. Spoon the batter into a greased or papered muffin tin. Fill each cup nearly to the top.

6. Bake for 15 to 20 minutes.

7. Cool the muffins at least 10 minutes before removing from the tin.

NUTRITIONAL FACTS (per 89-gram muffin)
Calories: 187 (14% from fat)

Fat: 3 g	Cholesterol: <1 mg	Carbohydrates: 32 g
Protein: 6 g	Fiber: 2.6 g	Sodium: 210 mg
Potassium: 369 mg	Iron: 2.0 mg	Calcium: 84 mg

White Chocolate and Raspberry Muffins

I'll never forget the first time I made these muffins. I was in Tennessee visiting my friends Nancy and Will. Heads hung over our plates, we bit into the still-warm-from-the-oven muffins. There was a prolonged pause, then a simultaneous, "Oh, my God!"

I have included these muffins in this chapter even though white chocolate is not chocolate at all—it's a combination of cocoa butter, milk, sugar, and vanilla. It makes no difference if you use white chocolate chunks or chips in this recipe, just be sure to chop it until it resembles a coarse powder. This allows the chocolate to melt into the muffin, spreading its delicious goodness throughout.

Dry Ingredients	Wet Ingredients
1 cup whole-wheat pastry flour	1¼ cups skim milk
1 cup unbleached white flour	½ cup nonfat sour cream
½ cup whole-wheat flour	2 large egg whites
¾ cup sugar	3 teaspoons vanilla extract
1½ teaspoons baking powder	
1 teaspoon baking soda	
¼ teaspoon sea salt	

Goodies

¾ cup firm fresh raspberries* (about 6 ounces), washed, patted dry, and halved

½ cup finely chopped (to a powder) white chocolate

* Can use frozen raspberries that have been thawed, drained, and patted dry.

Yield: 12 muffins

1. Preheat the oven to 400° F.

2. Sift the dry ingredients together in a large bowl. Add the goodies and toss to coat.

3. Whisk the wet ingredients in a medium bowl or blend them in a food processor. Pour the wet ingredients into the dry mixture. Stir just until mixed, taking care not to break the raspberries or cause their juice to color the batter. *Do not overstir.*

4. Spoon the batter into a greased or papered muffin tin. Fill each cup nearly to the top.

5. Bake for 15 to 20 minutes.

6. Cool the muffins at least 10 minutes before removing from the tin.

NUTRITIONAL FACTS (per 95-gram muffin)
Calories: 202 (11% from fat)

Fat: 3 g	Cholesterol: <1 mg	Carbohydrates: 39 g
Protein: 6 g	Fiber: 1.7 g	Sodium: 229 mg
Potassium: 178 mg	Iron: 1.0 mg	Calcium: 106 mg

6.

OVER-THE-TOP AND OUT-OF-THE-QUESTION MUFFINS

T he English have an expression—"over the top." It is generally used as an exclamation when an object or behavior is unrestrained, outrageous, flamboyant, extravagant, lavish, prohibitive, or excessive. I first heard this expression during a three-month retreat at a Buddhist monastery in England. There, a Thai woman named Net made a chocolate cake that contained an entire pound of grated dark Belgian chocolate! Can we talk? The cake was definitely "over the top."

Another expression—"out of the question"—first appeared in the early 1700s and generally refers to something that is unthinkable, impossible, foreign to the subject, or not worth considering. But I've taken to using this expression in the same manner as one might use "over the top." Net's chocolate cake was definitely "out of the question!"

When it came time for me to name this final chapter, these two expressions seemed to appropriately describe this special class of muffins. Here you will find muffins made with liqueurs, nuts, and exotic fruits. There are upside-down muffins, muffins crowned with delectable icings and glazes, and others created with holidays and other special occasions in mind. I think you will agree, they are all definitely "over the top" and right "out of the question."

Amaretto Muffins

I had wanted to make an amaretto-flavored muffin for some time, but I was never able to get the flavoring quite right. That is, not until flavored coffees became popular. That's when little bottles of interesting flavorings—amaretto, Irish cream, cappuccino, toasted pecan—began appearing on grocery store shelves near the coffee. Just a drop or two turns an ordinary cup of coffee into a coffee-bar masterpiece.

I used this type of flavoring in my Amaretto Muffins. Topped with sliced almonds, a sprinkling of pearl sugar crystals, and a cherry, these muffins are impressive to look at and even more impressive to taste. Without the almonds, these muffins have less than one gram of fat each. (Personally, I wouldn't leave the almonds out.)

Dry Ingredients	Wet Ingredients
1 cup whole-wheat flour	1 cup nonfat buttermilk
¾ cup unbleached white flour	½ cup water
¾ cup barley flour	¼ cup honey
½ cup sugar	2 large egg whites
1½ teaspoons baking powder	1½ teaspoons amaretto
1 teaspoon baking soda	flavoring
¼ teaspoon sea salt	

Goodies

¾ cup dark sweet cherries, pitted and chopped

Topping

½ cup sliced almonds

1 tablespoon pearl sugar crystals

Yield: 12 muffins

1. Preheat the oven to 400° F.

2. Sift the dry ingredients together in a large bowl.

3. Reserve 3 cherries (cut in quarters) to top each muffin (see Step 5). Add the remaining cherries to the dry ingredients and toss to coat.

4. Whisk the wet ingredients in a medium bowl or blend them in a food processor. Pour the wet ingredients into the dry mixture. Stir just until mixed. *Do not overstir.*

5. Spoon the batter into a greased or papered muffin tin. Fill each cup nearly to the top. Top each cup of batter with a large pinch of sliced almonds and a sprinkling of pearl sugar. Crown each with one of the reserved cherry quarters.

6. Bake for 15 to 20 minutes.

7. Cool the muffins at least 10 minutes before removing from the tin.

NUTRITIONAL FACTS (per 96-gram muffin)
Calories: 186 (15% from fat)

Fat: 3 g	Cholesterol: 0 mg	Carbohydrates: 36 g
Protein: 5 g	Fiber: 3.6 g	Sodium: 256 mg
Potassium: 165 mg	Iron: 1.1 mg	Calcium: 75 mg

Bananas Foster Muffins

Many years ago, my boyfriend and I dined at sunset on the fourteenth floor of a popular hotel in Asheville, North Carolina. The peaks of the Blue Ridge Mountains spread majestically across our entire field of vision. Like a Bargello tapestry, the mountains glimmered in the fading shades of blue from which their name is derived. At the far end of the candlelit room, love songs filled the air through the accomplished fingers of a grand pianist. And tableside, our waiter set brandy-soaked bananas aflame with a flamboyant gesture and a mischievous wink at the man and woman before him. My boyfriend, the Blue Ridge Mountains, love songs, and Bananas Foster. Ah, life is good.

Pristine moments like this one are a part of life's experience. They don't happen very often, do they? But when they do, they always make an indelible impression in our memory banks. Now, with my Bananas Foster Muffins, I am able to recall that wonderful evening and relive its sensory pleasures again and again. Ah, life is double good!

Dry Ingredients	Wet Ingredients
1 cup unbleached white flour	3 ripe bananas, mashed (1½ cups)
¼ cup whole-wheat pastry flour	¼ cup skim milk
½ cup whole-wheat flour	½ cup nonfat sour cream
¾ cup light brown sugar	1 large egg
1¼ teaspoons baking soda	3½ teaspoons brandy flavoring
1 teaspoon baking powder	1 teaspoon vanilla extract
¼ teaspoon sea salt	1 teaspoon grated lemon peel

Crunchy Topping

3 tablespoons honey-crunch wheat germ

Yield: 12–13 muffins

1. Preheat the oven to 375° F.

2. Sift the dry ingredients together in a large bowl.

3. Whisk the wet ingredients in a medium bowl or blend them in a food processor. Pour the wet ingredients into the dry ingredients. Stir just until mixed. *Do not overstir.*

4. Spoon the batter into a greased or papered muffin tin. Fill each cup nearly to the top. Top each muffin with about 1 teaspoon of wheat germ, taking care to spread it evenly over each cup.

5. Bake for 15 to 20 minutes.

6. Cool the muffins at least 10 minutes before removing from the tin.

NUTRITIONAL FACTS (per 96-gram muffin)
Calories: 176 (5% from fat)

Fat: 1 g	Cholesterol: 18 mg	Carbohydrates: 38 g
Protein: 5 g	Fiber: 2.2 g	Sodium: 226 mg
Potassium: 315 mg	Iron: 1.4 mg	Calcium: 79 mg

Blueberry Peach-Schnapps Muffins

It was a Sunday in July. My friend Linda and I found our way to our favorite spot for brunch—the Village Tavern in Winston-Salem. As we enjoyed our meal, shaded under one of the large canvas umbrellas that characterize the Tavern, our conversation turned to muffins. Linda had been describing a muffin recipe that featured her favorite ingredient—blueberries. I said one of the most felicitous acts of nature is the simultaneous ripening of peaches and blueberries. While it's true that individually their flavors stand out in a crowd, in combination . . . what can I say? It's perfection! Right then and there, I decided to create a muffin with peaches, blueberries, and peach schnapps.

Here are a few tips when making these sensational Blueberry Peach-Schnapps Muffins:

- *Select small, firm blueberries. They hold together better during the heat of baking.*
- *Use canned peaches packed in real fruit juice. I've tried making these muffins with fresh peaches, but I find them to be too acidic. The batter bubbles up and then goes flat.*
- *When applying the glaze, pull the muffins away from the sides of the muffin cups so the glaze can run down the sides and soak the entire muffin. Mmm.*

Dry Ingredients	Wet Ingredients
¾ cup whole-wheat pastry flour	¾ cup skim milk
½ cup whole-wheat flour	1 large egg
½ cup unbleached white flour	½ teaspoon lemon extract
½ cup sugar	
1½ teaspoons baking soda	
1 teaspoon baking powder	
½ teaspoon ground nutmeg	
¼ teaspoon sea salt	
1 cup oat or wheat bran	

Peach-Schnapps Glaze	Goodies
1 tablespoon light margarine	16-ounce can peaches packed
¼ cup sugar	in fruit juice, well drained
¼ cup peach schnapps	¾ cup firm fresh blueberries,
	washed and patted dry

Yield: 11–12 muffins

1. Preheat the oven to 375° F.

2. Sift all of the dry ingredients, except the oat or wheat bran, together in a large bowl. Add the bran and stir to combine. Add the blueberries and toss to coat.

3. Purée the peaches in a food processor or blender to yield about 1¼ cups purée. Add the wet ingredients and pulse to blend. (You can also use a fork or potato ricer to mash the peaches, then blend in the wet ingredients by hand.)

4. Pour the wet mixture into the dry mixture. Stir just until mixed. *Do not overstir.*

5. Spoon batter into greased or papered muffin tin. Fill each cup nearly to top.

6. Bake for 15 to 20 minutes.

7. While the muffins bake, prepare the glaze. Melt the margarine in a small saucepan over medium heat. Add the sugar and cook, stirring constantly, until the sugar begins to brown (about 5 minutes). Remove from heat and stir in the peach schnapps.

8. Remove the muffins from the oven. Using a skewer or toothpick, immediately pierce the top of each muffin in six or seven places. Drizzle the glaze evenly over each muffin until all of it is absorbed. Leave the muffins in the tin at least 20 minutes before removing.

NUTRITIONAL FACTS (per 93-gram muffin)
Calories: 182 (11% from fat)

Fat: 2 g	Cholesterol: 20 mg	Carbohydrates: 40 g
Protein: 5 g	Fiber: 3.2 g	Sodium: 264 mg
Potassium: 207 mg	Iron: 1.3 mg	Calcium: 67 mg

Butterscotch Pecan Muffins

The idea for this muffin grew out of my love for pecan pralines. I wanted to create a muffin with that nutty, burnt-sugar flavor. At first, I went to the trouble of making the pralines. I boiled the pecans in sugar water until they were brown and crispy, then I chopped them into bits. The muffins were delicious, but making the pralines from scratch was much too labor-intensive. My muffins had to be quick and easy to bake.

Soon thereafter, I had gone to the grocery store to get chocolate syrup for one of my muffin recipes when I noticed a fat-free butterscotch sundae syrup by Smuckers. "Hmm," I thought. "I can use that instead of pralines for my muffins. Butterscotch candies are very similar to pralines. They are made with brown sugar, corn syrup, and water. And using butterscotch syrup would certainly make these muffins easy to bake."

It worked. And I ask you—where else can you find a pecan muffin with only two grams of fat?

For an added touch, retain twelve or thirteen pecan quarters and place one on top of each muffin before baking.

Dry Ingredients	Wet Ingredients
1¼ cups whole-wheat flour	1¼ cups skim milk
1¼ cups unbleached white flour	½ cup fat-free butterscotch syrup
½ cup dark brown sugar	½ cup nonfat sour cream
1½ teaspoons baking soda	2 large egg whites
1 teaspoon baking powder	1 teaspoon vanilla
¼ teaspoon sea salt	

Goodies

½ cup chopped roasted pecans

Yield: 12–13 muffins

1. Preheat the oven to 400° F.

2. Sift the dry ingredients together in a large bowl. Add the pecans and stir to combine.

3. Whisk the wet ingredients in a medium bowl or blend them in a food processor. Pour the wet ingredients into the dry mixture. Stir just until mixed. *Do not overstir.*

4. Spoon the batter into a greased or papered muffin tin. Fill each cup nearly to the top.

5. Bake for 15 to 20 minutes.

6. Cool the muffins at least 10 minutes before removing from the tin.

NUTRITIONAL FACTS (per 85-gram muffin)
Calories: 192 (15% from fat)

Fat: 2 g	Cholesterol: <1 mg	Carbohydrates: 37 g
Protein: 5 g	Fiber: 2.3 g	Sodium: 251 mg
Potassium: 223 mg	Iron: 1.3 mg	Calcium: 78 mg

Caribbean Sweet-Potato Gingerbread Muffins

In **Gingerbread** (Simon and Schuster, 1989), author Linda Merinoff describes the many faces of gingerbread as it has traveled through time and across continents. She writes that islanders in the Caribbean used sweet potato purée as the base for gingerbread. "What a brilliant idea," I thought. Using sweet potatoes in baked goods makes perfect sense. They are a rich source of beta-carotene, vitamin C, vitamin B$_6$, fiber, iron, and potassium. Plus—and here's the best part—they are fat-free!

To make the purée called for in this recipe, first, drain a 16-ounce can of sweet potatoes, reserving the liquid. Then, in a food processor or blender, purée the potatoes with 1 cup of the reserved liquid. If necessary, add water to measure this amount. (You can also use a fork or potato ricer to mash the potatoes by hand.) Use what you need for this recipe and freeze the remaining purée for your next batch or make a double batch now!

Dry Ingredients	Wet Ingredients
1½ cups whole-wheat pastry flour	1 cup sweet potato purée
½ cup whole-wheat flour	(see above)
½ cup unbleached white flour	1 cup skim milk
½ cup dark brown sugar	¼ cup molasses
1½ teaspoons baking soda	2 large egg whites
1 teaspoon baking powder	2 teaspoons grated orange peel
1 teaspoon ground cinnamon	1 tablespoon grated fresh ginger
½ teaspoon ground cloves	(or 1½ teaspoons powdered)
¼ teaspoon ground nutmeg	
¼ teaspoon sea salt	

Yield: 12 muffins

1. Preheat the oven to 400° F.

2. Sift the dry ingredients together in a large bowl.

3. Whisk the wet ingredients in a medium bowl or blend them in a food processor. Pour the wet ingredients into the dry ingredients. Stir just until mixed. Do not overstir.

4. Spoon the batter into a greased or papered muffin tin. Fill each cup nearly to the top.

5. Bake for 15 to 20 minutes.

6. Cool the muffins at least 10 minutes before removing from the tin.

NUTRITIONAL FACTS (per 84-gram muffin)
Calories: 149 (3% from fat)

Fat: <1 g	Cholesterol: <1 mg	Carbohydrates: 34 g
Protein: 4 g	Fiber: 2.9 g	Sodium: 283 mg
Potassium: 265 mg	Iron: 1.9 mg	Calcium: 92 mg

Far East Muffins

*My nephew Ron is a martial artist. He is skilled in a Chinese form of karate—
kenpo kosho ryer—that dates back to the thirteenth century. One afternoon over
lunch, I had the opportunity to talk with Ron about kenpo.*

*I was interested in knowing what kenpo was like as well as what Ron got out
of it. He told me it was a very disciplined practice, kind of like meditation. While
it appears to be purely physical, it is as much mental in that it helps him control
his mind while he controls his body.*

*I was happy for Ron and his growing interest in mastering this ancient Asian
art form. He felt and sounded relaxed and serene—as if he had just completed a
long meditation retreat or returned from a relaxing vacation. Ron was definitely
enjoying inner and outer harmony.*

*Here is a muffin for you, Ron. Made with a blend of spices from the part of
the world that gave birth to kenpo, these muffins are timeless. You might enjoy
them topped with vanilla or lemon yogurt-cheese icing (see Making Yogurt-
Cheese Icing beginning on page 168).*

Dry Ingredients	Wet Ingredients
1 cup whole-wheat pastry flour	1 cup low-fat vanilla yogurt
1 cup brown rice flour	½ cup skim milk
½ cup unbleached white flour	½ cup honey
1½ teaspoons baking soda	2 large egg whites
1 teaspoon baking powder	2 tablespoons finely chopped
½ teaspoon ground cardamom	fresh ginger root
¼ teaspoon ground cinnamon	2 teaspoons grated lemon peel
⅛ teaspoon ground clove	
¼ teaspoon sea salt	

Yield: 12 muffins

1. Preheat the oven to 400° F.

2. Sift the dry ingredients together in a large bowl.

3. Whisk the wet ingredients in a medium bowl or blend them in a food processor. Pour the wet ingredients into the dry ingredients. Stir just until mixed. *Do not overstir.*

4. Spoon the batter into a greased or papered muffin tin. Fill each cup nearly to the top.

5. Bake for 15 to 20 minutes.

6. Cool the muffins at least 10 minutes before removing from the tin.

NUTRITIONAL FACTS (per 89-gram muffin)
Calories: 158 (2% from fat)

Fat: <1 g	Cholesterol: 1 mg	Carbohydrates: 35 g
Protein: 5 g	Fiber: 1.2 g	Sodium: 266 mg
Potassium: 213 mg	Iron: 0.9 mg	Calcium: 108 mg

Flipped Apple Muffins

Here's an apple muffin that is moist beyond belief. The juicy sweet "topping" with just a hint of rum permeates the muffins with fruit juices while they bake. When the muffins are removed from the oven and flipped upside down on a serving platter, the remaining fruit juice soaks through the muffins and down their sides as they cool. Sliced apples grace the "top" like a crown, making an impressive presentation for any occasion.

These muffins, which are reminiscent of apple turnovers or dumplings, are great for breakfast. They are also great for dessert with a scoop of low-fat vanilla ice cream or frozen yogurt and, perhaps, a drizzle of fat-free butterscotch syrup.

Please be aware that the liquid "topping" in these muffins tends to boil up and overflow during baking. Be sure to put a tray underneath the tin to catch the overflowing liquid and spare your oven.

Dry Ingredients	Wet Ingredients
1 cup whole-wheat flour	¾ cup skim milk
1 cup unbleached white flour	½ cup applesauce
1½ teaspoons baking soda	½ cup honey
1 teaspoon baking powder	2 large egg whites
1 teaspoon ground cinnamon	2 teaspoons grated lemon peel
¼ teaspoon sea salt	1 teaspoon vanilla extract
1 cup oat bran	

"Topping"	
1 tablespoon light margarine	3 small apples, cut lengthwise
½ cup brown sugar	into ¼-inch slices
½ cup apple juice	2 teaspoons rum flavoring

Yield: 12 muffins

1. Preheat the oven to 375° F.

2. To prepare the topping, melt the margarine in a small saucepan over medium heat. Add the sugar and cook, stirring frequently, until the sugar begins to brown (about 5 minutes). Add the apple juice and sliced apples and cook 5 minutes. Remove from the heat and stir in the rum flavoring.

3. Grease the cups of a muffin tin and place 3 or 4 cooked apple slices in the bottom of each. Pour even amounts of the juice in each cup (should measure a little less than 1 tablespoon per cup.) Set the prepared muffin tin aside.

4. Sift all of the dry ingredients, except the oat bran, together in a large bowl. Add the oat bran and stir to combine.

5. Whisk the wet ingredients in a medium bowl or blend them in a food processor. Pour the wet ingredients into the dry ingredients. Stir just until mixed. *Do not overstir.*

6. Spoon the batter into the prepared muffin tin. Fill each cup nearly to the top.

7. Bake for 15 to 20 minutes.

8. When the muffins are done, immediately turn them upside down on a platter or baking sheet. *Do not remove the muffin tin.* Allow the muffins to cool in this position at least 10 minutes before removing the tin. (You may need the help of a knife to free the muffins.)

NUTRITIONAL FACTS (per 113-gram muffin)
Calories: 198 (7% from fat)

Fat: 2 g	Cholesterol: <1 mg	Carbohydrates: 46 g
Protein: 5 g	Fiber: 3.3 g	Sodium: 249 mg
Potassium: 241 mg	Iron: 1.6 mg	Calcium: 69 mg

When All Else Fails, Follow the Directions

My sister Diane telephoned one day to tell me that her favorite muffins from my first book were the Eat Your Oatmeal Muffins. She said she was making a batch just about every other week and loved them. "However," she said, "the kids thought the last batch I made was a little heavy." She wondered why.

"Well," I said, "describe how you made them." I could hear her turning the pages of my book to find the recipe.

"Well, first of all I guess I better tell you that I didn't have any whole-wheat pastry flour so I used a mixture of whole-wheat and white."

"That's fine," I said. "Did you find that you needed to adjust the liquid?"

"Well, yeah—especially to absorb the cereal."

"What cereal?" I asked.

"Oh, I forgot to tell you about that. I ran out of rolled oats, so I pulverized some stale Wheaties."

"I see."

"And then there was the thing with the apples."

"What about the apples?"

"I didn't have any, so I used some canned fruit

cocktail instead."

"Diane! Is there anything else you want to tell me?"

"Just the applesauce."

"Huh?"

"Well, I didn't have any apple-juice concentrate, so I used some watered-down applesauce instead."

"Gee, Diane, I wonder why the muffins didn't come out right . . . "

Gingerbread Muffins with Lemon Curd Filling

If you've ever spread lemon curd—a popular English dessert filling—on gingerbread, you'll know why I created these muffins. Like peanut butter and jelly, lemon curd and gingerbread were made for each other.

The lemon curd filling melts into the muffins as they bake. If you open one of these muffins before it has cooled, you'll find a hole in the center where the lemon curd used to be. As the muffin cools, however, the curd magically reappears.

These days, fresh ginger root, which is called for in this recipe, is readily available in most grocery stores. However, if you have difficulty finding it, simply add another ½ teaspoon of ground ginger to the dry ingredients. Finding lemon curd is another matter. I have found that the smaller grocery stores tend not to carry it. Look for lemon curd in the imported food aisle or in the jams and jelly section of larger grocery stores. I have even seen it stocked with the pie fillings and cake ingredients.

Dry Ingredients	Wet Ingredients
1½ cups whole-wheat flour	1½ cups nonfat buttermilk
1 cup unbleached white flour	½ cup molasses
½ cup light brown sugar	2 large egg whites
1½ teaspoons baking soda	1½ tablespoons grated orange peel
1 teaspoon baking powder	1½ tablespoons finely chopped
1½ tablespoons ground ginger	fresh ginger root
1½ teaspoons ground cinnamon	
1 teaspoon ground nutmeg	
¼ teaspoon sea salt	

Goodies

⅜–½ cup lemon curd

Yield: 12 muffins

1. Preheat the oven to 400° F.

2. Sift the dry ingredients together in a large bowl.

3. Whisk the wet ingredients in a medium bowl or blend them in a food processor. Pour the wet ingredients into the dry ingredients. Stir just until mixed. *Do not overstir.*

4. Spoon half the batter into greased or papered muffin cups. Place 1 teaspoon of lemon curd on top of the batter in the center of each cup. Spoon the remaining batter into the cups, enclosing the lemon curd.

5. Bake for 15 to 20 minutes.

6. Cool the muffins at least 10 minutes before removing from the tin.

NUTRITIONAL FACTS (per 95-gram muffin)
Calories: 216 (2% from fat)

Fat: 1 g	Cholesterol: 0 mg	Carbohydrates: 50 g
Protein: 5 g	Fiber: 2.5 g	Sodium: 321 mg
Potassium: 270 mg	Iron: 2.5 mg	Calcium: 113 mg

Grand Marnier Creamsicle Muffins

The spell-check function on my computer doesn't like the word Marnier. Every time it comes upon the word it asks, "Are you sure you don't mean 'mariner'?" (Neither does it like the Sanskrit and Pali words it comes across when I spell check my Buddhist meditation stories. Every time the program encounters 'bhikkhu,' the ancient Pali word for monk, it asks, "Are you sure you don't mean 'buckaroo'?" The monks would certainly get a kick out of that.)

Hmm. Mariner. I watch as my mind flashes through its mariner file—Rime of the Ancient Mariner, The Ghost and Mrs. Muir, the sea captain in Mary Poppins. I hear Gordon Lightfoot singing "The Wreck of the Edmund Fitzgerald." And for a moment (thanks to my Macintosh Classic II), I doubt my spelling. I get up, walk to the kitchen sink, open the cupboard below, and—for the third time while writing this book—check the label on the bottle of Grand Marnier. Oh computers—the power of these little boxes of silicone crystals and circuitry. How easily they can make us doubt what we know!

I use Grand Marnier in these muffins because it is my personal favorite. But you can use whatever orange-flavored liqueur you choose. Your computer's spell-check may have an easier time with another selection.

Dry Ingredients	Wet Ingredients
1¼ cups whole-wheat flour	1 cup skim milk
1 cup unbleached white flour	½ cup nonfat sour cream
½ cup brown rice flour	½ cup honey
1½ teaspoons baking powder	¼ cup orange-juice concentrate
1 teaspoon baking soda	2 large egg whites
¼ teaspoon sea salt	2 tablespoons grated orange peel
	1½ teaspoons vanilla extract

Grand Marnier Glaze

1 tablespoon light margarine   ¼ cup Grand Marnier liqueur
¼ cup sugar

Yield: 12 muffins

1. Preheat the oven to 375° F.

2. Sift the dry ingredients together in a large bowl.

3. Whisk the wet ingredients in a medium bowl or blend them in a food processor. Pour the wet ingredients into the dry ingredients. Stir just until mixed. *Do not overstir.*

4. Spoon the batter into a greased or papered muffin tin. Fill each cup nearly to the top.

5. Bake for 15 to 20 minutes.

6. While the muffins bake, prepare the glaze. Melt the margarine in a small saucepan over medium heat. Add the sugar and cook, stirring constantly, until the sugar begins to brown (about 5 minutes). Remove from the heat and stir in the Grand Marnier.

7. Remove the muffins from the oven. Using a skewer or toothpick, immediately pierce the top of each muffin in six or seven places. Drizzle the glaze evenly over each muffin until all of it is absorbed. Leave the muffins in the tin at least 20 minutes before removing.

NUTRITIONAL FACTS (per 89-gram muffin)
Calories: 197 (5% from fat)

Fat: 1 g	Cholesterol: <1 mg	Carbohydrates: 42 g
Protein: 5 g	Fiber: 2.0 g	Sodium: 224 mg
Potassium: 227 mg	Iron: 1.2 mg	Calcium: 90 mg

Hillsborough House Inn Breakfast Muffins

I first met Katherine and Bev Webb, owners of the Hillsborough House Inn, while on the 1994 Christmas tour of homes in historic Hillsborough, North Carolina. As I stepped onto the 80-foot long front porch of this magnificent home (circa 1790), I sensed the presence of the many residents and visitors who had climbed the stairs before me. Inside I found cozy, romantic, candlelit parlors and bedrooms with family and historic memorabilia everywhere in sight.

When, months later, I stayed at the Inn and was able to experience Katherine and Bev's hospitality firsthand, that settled it. I had to create a muffin especially for them—one with a little bit of North Carolina (the sweet potato capital of the world), a little bit of old country magic (currants), and lots of the sweet joy of friendship.

For instructions on preparing sweet potato purée, see Caribbean Sweet-Potato Gingerbread Muffins on page 198.

Dry Ingredients	Wet Ingredients
1 cup whole-wheat pastry flour	1 cup sweet potato purée
½ cup whole-wheat flour	1 cup skim milk
½ cup unbleached white flour	¼ cup molasses
1½ teaspoons baking soda	2 large egg whites
1 teaspoon baking powder	2 teaspoons grated orange peel
¼ cup dark brown sugar	
1 teaspoon ground cinnamon	
½ teaspoon ground cloves	
¼ teaspoon ground nutmeg	
¼ teaspoon sea salt	
½ cup oat or wheat bran	

Topping	Goodies
½ cup honey-crunch wheat germ	½ cup currants
¼ cup coarsely chopped roasted walnuts	
¼ cup dark brown sugar	
1 tablespoon light margarine, melted	

Yield: 12 muffins

1. Preheat the oven to 400° F.

2. Prepare the topping by combining the wheat germ, nuts, and brown sugar in a small bowl. Add the margarine and stir to combine. Set aside.

3. Sift all of the dry ingredients, except the oat or wheat bran, together in a large bowl. Add the bran and stir to combine.

4. Whisk the wet ingredients in a medium bowl or blend them in a food processor. Add the currants and stir to combine. Pour the wet mixture into the dry mixture. Stir just until mixed. *Do not overstir.*

5. Spoon the batter into a greased or papered muffin tin. Fill each cup nearly to the top. Top each cup of batter with the prepared topping, taking care to spread it evenly over each cup. Too much topping piled in the middle will prevent the muffins from rising properly.

6. Bake for 15 to 20 minutes.

7. Cool the muffins at least 10 minutes before removing from the tin.

NUTRITIONAL FACTS (per 91-gram muffin)
Calories: 193 (15% from fat)

Fat: 3 g	Cholesterol: <1 mg	Carbohydrates: 36 g
Protein: 7 g	Fiber: 4.2 g	Sodium: 280 mg
Potassium: 346 mg	Iron: 2.6 mg	Calcium: 98 mg

Mango with Crystallized Ginger Muffins

Mangoes are my favorite fruit. Sorry bananas. Sorry peaches. Sorry blueberries. You are wonderful but, I am afraid, wholly and utterly forgotten the minute I bite into a mango. In addition to its stop-the-world flavor, the mango is a rich source of vitamins, particularly vitamin C. It is also packed with beta-carotene, potassium, and fiber, and contains only about 100 calories.

Apparently mangoes didn't always taste as wonderful as they do today. Through my research, I discovered that mangoes originally tasted a lot like turpentine, but centuries of cultivation have produced the succulent, sweet fruit we enjoy today.

One of my favorite ways to enjoy a mango is sliced with a light sprinkling of freshly grated ginger root. That's what inspired these muffins. I hope you enjoy them!

Dry Ingredients:	Wet Ingredients:
1¾ cups whole-wheat flour	1¼ cups skim milk
1½ cups unbleached white flour	½ cup honey
¼ cup light brown sugar	1 large egg
2 teaspoons baking soda	1 teaspoon rum flavoring
1 teaspoon baking powder	1 teaspoon grated lemon peel
¼ teaspoon sea salt	

Goodies

3 tablespoons coarsely chopped crystallized ginger
16-ounce can mango, well drained (or enough fresh mango to yield
  1 cup purée)

Yield: 12 muffins

1. Preheat the oven to 375° F.

2. Sift the dry ingredients together in a large bowl. Add the crystallized ginger and toss to coat.

3. Purée the mangoes in a food processor or blender to yield about 1 cup. Add the remaining wet ingredients and pulse to blend. (You can also use a fork or potato ricer to mash the mangoes, then blend in the wet ingredients by hand.)

4. Pour the wet mixture into the dry mixture. Stir just until mixed. *Do not overstir.*

5. Spoon the batter into a greased or papered muffin tin. Fill each cup nearly to the top.

6. Bake for 15 to 20 minutes.

7. Cool the muffins at least 10 minutes before removing from the tin.

NUTRITIONAL FACTS (per 93-gram muffin)
Calories: 202 (4% from fat)

Fat: 1 g	Cholesterol: 18 mg	Carbohydrates: 45 g
Protein: 5 g	Fiber: 2.9 g	Sodium: 192 mg
Potassium: 208 mg	Iron: 1.5 mg	Calcium: 76 mg

Patty's Reincarnated Cappuccino Muffins

My friend Patty loves the cappuccino muffins from my first book so much that she has single-handedly consumed about two dozen a month for the past two years! It was only fitting that I name this new lower-fat version for her. Patty has personally tested and approved them. (And believe me, she's an expert.)

Read through the following tips. I have offered them to help ensure this recipe's sucess:

- *For best results, use brewed coffee made with freshly ground coffee beans. Use about 2¼ tablespoons of ground coffee to make ¾ cup of triple-strength brew.*
- *To facilitate blending, add the honey while the coffee is hot.*
- *Cool the brew to room temperature before adding the remaining wet ingredients.*
- *If you are in a hurry and don't have time to brew fresh coffee, simply add 2¼ teaspoons instant coffee to ¾ cup of lukewarm water.*
- *Blend the wet ingredients very well. I use a food processor, but you can also use an electric mixer or wire whisk. It's important to blend the ingredients well or you may end up with clumps of sour cream throughout the muffins.*

Dry Ingredients	Wet Ingredients
1½ cups unbleached white flour	¾ cup triple-strength coffee, cooled to room temperature
1 cup whole-wheat flour	¾ cup nonfat sour cream
½ cup light brown sugar	½ cup honey
1½ teaspoons baking soda	2 large egg whites
1 teaspoon baking powder	1 teaspoon vanilla extract
3 tablespoons cocoa powder	
1 teaspoon ground cinnamon	
¼ teaspoon sea salt	

Yield: 12 muffins

1. Preheat the oven to 400° F.

2. Sift the dry ingredients together in a large bowl.

3. Whisk the wet ingredients in a medium bowl or blend them in a food processor. Pour the wet ingredients into the dry ingredients. Stir just until mixed. *Do not overstir.*

4. Spoon the batter into a greased or papered muffin tin. Fill each cup nearly to the top.

5. Bake for 15 to 20 minutes.

6. Cool the muffins at least 10 minutes before removing from the tin.

NUTRITIONAL FACTS (per 72-gram muffin)
Calories: 184 (2% from fat)

Fat: <1 g	Cholesterol: 0 mg	Carbohydrates: 42 g
Protein: 5 g	Fiber: 2.1 g	Sodium: 255 mg
Potassium: 250 mg	Iron: 1.8 mg	Calcium: 61 mg

Pineapple Carrot Ginger Muffins

"What do you consider to be truly essential in life, Gloria? I mean what is critical to your survival?"

"Well, there are hot fudge sundaes, baked brie with almonds, tahini, maple vanilla yogurt, and carrot cake. Surely, one can't expect to survive without these!"

But with an expanding middle-age waistline and clothes that don't want to fit, how do I justify eating traditional carrot cake with butter and cream cheese icing and those very fattening macadamia nuts? The answer is: I don't. I can't. I won't (at least not very often). To satisfy the "need" for carrot cake without the fat, I have created Pineapple Carrot Ginger Muffins, which contain only 2 grams of fat each. Try topping these muffins with the Nonfat Cream-Cheese Icing on page 174. With or without the icing, the fat content is the same.

Dry Ingredients	Wet Ingredients
1¼ cups whole-wheat flour	1½ cups skim milk
1¼ cups unbleached white flour	¼ cup apple-juice concentrate
½ cup light brown sugar	1 large egg
1½ teaspoons baking soda	1 tablespoon canola oil
1 teaspoon baking powder	1 teaspoon grated orange peel
1 teaspoon powdered ginger	
¼ teaspoon sea salt	

Goodies

½ cup grated carrots
½ cup chopped dried pineapple
2 tablespoons grated ginger root

Yield: 11–12 muffins

1. Preheat the oven to 400° F.

2. Sift the dry ingredients together in a large bowl. Add the goodies to the dry ingredients and toss to coat.

3. Whisk the wet ingredients in a medium bowl or blend them in a food processor. Pour the wet ingredients into the dry mixture. Stir just until mixed. *Do not overstir.*

4. Spoon the batter into a greased or papered muffin tin. Fill each cup nearly to the top.

5. Bake for 15 to 20 minutes.

6. Cool the muffins at least 10 minutes before removing from the tin.

NUTRITIONAL FACTS (per 92-gram muffin)
Calories: 165 (11% from fat)

Fat: 2 g	Cholesterol: 18 mg	Carbohydrates: 33 g
Protein: 5 g	Fiber: 2.2 g	Sodium: 250 mg
Potassium: 242 mg	Iron: 1.4 mg	Calcium: 83 mg

Pineapple Upside-Down Muffins

Upside-down muffins are twice the fun of right-side-up muffins. First, there's the fun of creatively filling the bottom of each muffin cup with the goodies that will eventually be on top. Then there's the added kick of flipping the tin over and witnessing the results of your artistry. Your family and friends will be dazzled when they see that you've turned this traditional tropical favorite into muffins. (If you like these muffins, you might like to try the Flipped Apple Muffins on page 202).

Here are a few tips: When you drain the pineapple for the "topping," reserve the juice to use in the wet ingredients. This will extend that pineapple goodness throughout the muffins. And when you put the crushed pineapple in the bottom of each cup, be sure to distribute it evenly. This way each bite will be filled with pineapple.

Dry Ingredients	Wet Ingredients
1½ cups whole-wheat flour	1 cup applesauce
1 cup whole-wheat pastry flour	½ cup nonfat buttermilk
¼ cup light brown sugar	½ cup water
1½ teaspoon baking soda	¼ cup pineapple juice
1 teaspoon baking powder	2 large egg whites
¼ teaspoon sea salt	2 teaspoons grated lemon peel
1 teaspoon vanilla extract	

"Topping"

¼ cup light margarine, melted

¼ cup light brown sugar

8-ounce can crushed pineapple, well drained

Yield: 12 muffins

1. Preheat the oven to 375° F.

2. After greasing the muffin tin, add the "toppings." First, place 1 teaspoon of melted margarine in the bottom of each cup. Next, add a teaspoon of brown sugar, distributing it evenly on the bottom. Spoon a heaping teaspoon of crushed pineapple into each cup, spreading it evenly over the brown sugar. Set the muffin tin aside.

3. Sift the dry ingredients together in a large bowl.

4. Whisk the wet ingredients in a medium bowl or blend them in a food processor. Pour the wet ingredients into the dry ingredients. Stir just until mixed. *Do not overstir.*

5. Spoon the batter into the prepared muffin tin. Fill each cup nearly to the top.

6. Bake for 15 to 20 minutes.

7. When the muffins are done, immediately turn them upside down on a platter or baking sheet. *Do not remove the muffin tin.* Allow the muffins to cool in this position at least 10 minutes before removing the tin. (You may need the help of a knife to free the muffins.)

NUTRITIONAL FACTS (per 96-gram muffin)
Calories: 155 (18% from fat)

Fat: 3 g	Cholesterol: 0 mg	Carbohydrates: 29 g
Protein: 4 g	Fiber: 3.0 g	Sodium: 270 mg
Potassium: 192 mg	Iron: 1.1 mg	Calcium: 61 mg

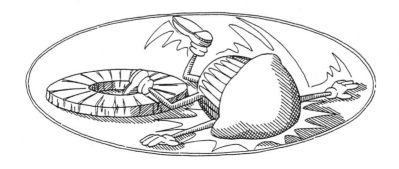

Pistachio and Dried Cranberry Muffins

In preparation for the final testing of these muffins, I went to my local market to buy the nuts. I was disappointed, however, to discover that, unlike my last visit (around Christmas-time when someone had done the work of shelling the nuts), these pistachios were still in their shells.

"What happened?" I asked the attendant. "You used to carry shelled pistachios."

"Those are shelled pistachios," replied the attendant.

"No," I said. "I mean shelled pistachios . . . the kind that have had the no shells."

"Those are unshelled pistachios, not shelled. And we don't carry them anymore."

I stared at her—paralyzed. It was one of those moments when I didn't know which expression was correct. What she was saying made sense, but . . . Could she be right? Could I have been saying it wrong all these years? As I scrambled to right a world that had suddenly been turned on its head, I remembered the pitted cherry. You know—the one that has had its pit removed. "And shelled pistachios are pistachios that have had their shells removed," I said to myself. Everyone knows that. When pistachios are in their shells they are just plain pistachios. When they have had their shells removed, they become shelled pistachios. The addition of the adjective says that the nuts have been acted upon in some way. They have been shelled. I shell. You shell. He shells. She shells. Right?

Rather than discuss it further with the attendant, I paid for my $7.99-a-pound "shelled" pistachios and went home to look it up. Guess which expression is correct.

Dry Ingredients	Wet Ingredients
1¾ cups unbleached white flour	1 cup skim milk
1 cup whole-wheat flour	½ cups nonfat sour cream
1½ teaspoons baking powder	½ cup honey
1 teaspoon baking soda	¼ cup apple-juice concentrate
¼ teaspoon sea salt	2 large egg whites
	1 teaspoon vanilla extract
	1 teaspoon grated orange peel

Goodies	Topping
¾ cup dried cranberries	1 egg white
	⅜ cup chopped roasted pistachios

Yield: 12 muffins

1. Preheat the oven to 400° F.

2. Sift the dry ingredients together in a large bowl.

3. Whisk the wet ingredients in a medium bowl or blend them in a food processor. Add the cranberries and stir to combine.

4. Pour the wet mixture into the dry ingredients. Stir just until mixed. *Do not overstir.*

5. Spoon the batter into a greased or papered muffin tin. Fill each cup nearly to the top.

6. Prepare the topping. Whip the egg white until it forms stiff peaks, then add the pistachios and stir to coat completely. Top each cup of batter with a heaping teaspoon of the topping, taking care to spread it evenly over each cup. Too much topping piled in the middle will prevent the muffins from rising properly.

7. Bake for 15 to 20 minutes.

8. Cool the muffins at least 10 minutes before removing from the tin.

NUTRITIONAL FACTS (per 95-gram muffin)
Calories: 198 (14% from fat)

Fat: 3 g	Cholesterol: <1 mg	Carbohydrates: 39 g
Protein: 6 g	Fiber: 2.6 g	Sodium: 219 mg
Potassium: 244 mg	Iron: 1.4 mg	Calcium: 88 mg

Rum Raisin Muffins

Made with the fabulous flavors of eggnog, these muffins can accompany any holiday meal. Along with a hot cup of Earl Grey tea, they are a great way to start the day. As a lunchtime dessert, enjoy them topped with a scoop of low-fat rum raisin ice cream or fat-free French vanilla frozen yogurt. At the holiday banquet, serve these muffins alongside the turkey or ham. Your family and guests will love you for it.

I use golden raisins in this recipe because I like their light color and flavor, but feel free to use dark raisins or even currants if you like. To give these muffins more of a fruitcake effect, use a combination of dried fruits instead of raisins only. May I suggest apricots, pineapple, and golden raisins?

Dry Ingredients	Wet Ingredients
1½ cups whole-wheat flour	1 cup low-fat vanilla yogurt
¾ cups unbleached white flour	1 cup water
½ cup light brown sugar	½ cup applesauce
1¼ teaspoon baking soda	1 large egg
½ teaspoon baking powder	2½ teaspoons rum flavoring
1 teaspoon ground nutmeg	1½ teaspoons grated lemon peel
¼ teaspoon ground cardamom	1 teaspoon vanilla extract
¼ teaspoon sea salt	

Goodies

1 cup golden raisins

Yield: 12 muffins

1. Preheat the oven to 400° F.

2. Sift the dry ingredients together in a large bowl.

3. Whisk the wet ingredients in a medium bowl or blend them in a food processor. Add the raisins to the wet ingredients and stir to combine.

4. Pour the wet mixture into the dry ingredients. Stir just until mixed. *Do not overstir.*

5. Spoon the batter into a greased or papered muffin tin. Fill each cup nearly to the top.

6. Bake for 15 to 20 minutes.

7. Cool the muffins at least 10 minutes before removing from the tin.

NUTRITIONAL FACTS (per 99-gram muffin)
Calories: 175 (5% from fat)

Fat: 1 g	Cholesterol: 18 mg	Carbohydrates: 39 g
Protein: 5 g	Fiber: 2.7 g	Sodium: 256 mg
Potassium: 282 mg	Iron: 1.4 mg	Calcium: 73 mg

Standard Spice Muffins with Vanilla Yogurt-Cheese Icing

There's a cupboard to the right of my kitchen sink where I keep my dishes, glasses, and coffee mugs. On the outside of this cabinet, on the side facing the sink, I nailed my thirty-six bottle spice rack. I don't know how I ended up with so many bottles of spices. When I first started cooking, I was perfectly satisfied with a twelve-bottle spice rack. A few years later—it must have been when I started cooking Asian foods—I replaced the twelve bottles with an eighteen-bottle set. This was getting serious. Before long, I noticed I was coveting my neighbors' spice racks—there was Deb's twenty-bottle wooden rack that swiveled and spun on the countertop, and Maury and Grethe's deluxe wall cabinet rack that unfolded into a multilayered, multileveled spice junkie's dream. And I found myself spending more than the usual amount of time in kitchenware departments and gourmet specialty shops.

I can't imagine life without spice. I use it everywhere—in my tea, on my toast, in Asian and other ethnic-style dishes, and certainly in muffins. When it comes to muffins, I like those with spice best. Here's a special muffin which, even when iced, contains only one gram of fat per muffin.

Dry Ingredients	Wet Ingredients
1¼ cups whole-wheat flour	1¼ cups nonfat buttermilk
1 cup whole-wheat pastry flour	1 cup applesauce
½ cup dark brown sugar	¼ cup honey
1 teaspoon baking powder	1 large egg
1 teaspoon baking soda	2 teaspoons grated orange peel
1 teaspoon ground cinnamon	
½ teaspoon ground nutmeg	
½ teaspoon ground ginger	
¼ teaspoon sea salt	
¼ cup oat bran	

Goodies	Vanilla Yogurt-Cheese Icing
¾ cup golden raisins	1 cup powdered sugar, sifted
	½ cup yogurt cheese (*see* page 168)
	1 teaspoon vanilla extract

Yield: 12 muffins

1. Preheat the oven to 375° F.

2. Sift all of the dry ingredients, except the oat bran, together in a large bowl. Add the oat bran and stir to combine.

3. Whisk the wet ingredients in a medium bowl or blend them in a food processor. Add the raisins to the wet ingredients and stir to combine.

4. Pour the wet mixture into the dry ingredients. Stir just until mixed. *Do not overstir.*

5. Spoon the batter into a greased or papered muffin tin. Fill each cup nearly to the top.

6. Bake for 15 to 20 minutes.

7. While the muffins bake, prepare the icing. With a spoon, stir the powdered sugar, yogurt cheese, and vanilla extract to an icing consistency. Do not use a food processor, blender, or electric mixer. Cover and refrigerate the icing until ready to use.

8. Cool the muffins at least 10 minutes before removing from the tin. Allow them to cool to room temperature before frosting.

NUTRITIONAL FACTS (per 123-gram muffin)
Calories: 225 (4% from fat)

Fat: 1 g	Cholesterol: 18 mg	Carbohydrates: 52 g
Protein: 6 g	Fiber: 3.6 g	Sodium: 227 mg
Potassium: 309 mg	Iron: 1.5 mg	Calcium: 125 mg

Sugar Plum Fairy Muffins

As far as sugar plum fairies go, my niece Annie wins the prize. An accomplished ballerina, Annie has made a habit over the years of attending as many performances of the "Nutcracker Suite" as her time and purse allow. (She loves this ballet so much that she decorates her Christmas tree with an ever-expanding collection of ornaments that are centered around the "Nutcracker" theme.) I have to say that when we went together to last year's performance at Lincoln Center for the Performing Arts, I experienced as much pleasure observing Annie's delight as I did watching the performance itself.

Here's a muffin that matches the lightness and agility of the dance of the sugar plum fairies and is as pleasing to the eye and heart as Annie. The combination of nonfat sour cream, applesauce, orange peel, and lemon peel gives this muffin its light and fruity appeal. Plum preserves and crystal sugar make the perfect topper. I use Garner's Damson Preserves, which has an especially rich homemade flavor. If you can't find Garner's (made in Winston-Salem, North Carolina) or any other brand of plum preserves, use plain old grape jam (not jelly).

Dry Ingredients	Wet Ingredients
1 cup whole-wheat flour	1 cup water
¾ cup unbleached white flour	¼ cup applesauce
½ cup brown rice flour	¾ cup nonfat sour cream
¼ cup sugar	2 large egg whites
1¼ teaspoons baking soda	1 teaspoon vanilla extract
1 teaspoon baking powder	1½ teaspoon grated orange peel
¼ teaspoon sea salt	2 teaspoons grated lemon peel

Glaze Topping	
¼ cup water	¼ cup plum preserves
1½ teaspoons cornstarch	2 tablespoons pearl sugar crystals

Yield: 11–12 muffins

1. Preheat the oven to 375° F.

2. Sift the dry ingredients together in a large bowl.

3. Whisk the wet ingredients in a medium bowl or blend them in a food processor. Pour the wet ingredients into the dry ingredients. Stir just until mixed. *Do not overstir.*

4. Spoon the batter into a greased or papered muffin tin. Fill each cup nearly to the top.

5. Bake for 15 to 20 minutes.

6. While the muffins bake, prepare the glaze. Place the water and cornstarch in a small saucepan and stir to dissolve any lumps. Add the plum preserves. Heat the mixture over medium-high heat, stirring frequently until it thickens (about 3 minutes). Remove from heat and set aside to cool.

7. Cool the muffins at least 10 minutes before removing from the tin.

8. When the muffins have cooled to room temperature, spoon about a teaspoon of glaze on each, smoothing it evenly on top. Sprinkle each with a large pinch of sugar crystals. (The glaze will harden a little as it continues to cool.)

NUTRITIONAL FACTS (per 104-gram muffin)
Calories: 165 (2% from fat)

Fat: <1 g	Cholesterol: 0 mg	Carbohydrates: 26 g
Protein: 5 g	Fiber: 2.1 g	Sodium: 245 mg
Potassium: 173 mg	Iron: 1.0 mg	Calcium: 56 mg

Triple-Apricot Ambrosia Muffins

The clerk at the checkout counter looked at the name on my charge card. "Ambrosia . . . what a delicious name! I just love ambrosia salad, don't you?" I assured her that I did, although I hadn't made it in a long time.

"I make mine with oranges and coconut. How do you make yours?" she asked.

"Well, I used to make it that way—that is, until I discovered how delicious it is with fresh apricots and just a hint of orange," I replied. "Try it. I think you'll like it."

My Triple Apricot Ambrosia Muffins match my ambrosia salad. Rich in fruity flavor and topped with a big pinch of flaked coconut, they contain only two grams of fat per muffin. If you want to reduce the fat in these muffins even further, eliminate the coconut from the dry ingredients (Step 2). Made this way, each muffin contains less than 1 gram of fat.

Dry Ingredients	Wet Ingredients
1 cup unbleached white flour	¾ cup skim milk
½ cup whole-wheat flour	2 large egg whites
½ cup brown rice flour	1 teaspoon grated orange peel
½ cup light brown sugar	
1 teaspoon baking powder	
1 teaspoon baking soda	
¼ teaspoon sea salt	

Goodies	
1 cup dried apricots, chopped	16-ounce can apricots packed
½ cup flaked coconut	in fruit juice, well drained

Topping

¼ cup all-fruit apricot preserves   ½ cup flaked coconut

Yield: 12 muffins

1. Preheat the oven to 375° F.

2. Sift all of the dry ingredients together in a large bowl. Add the dried apricots and coconut from the goody list and toss to coat.

3. Purée the canned apricots in a food processor or blender to yield about 1 cup purée. Add the wet ingredients and pulse to blend. (You can also use a fork or potato ricer to mash the apricots, then blend in the wet ingredients by hand.)

4. Pour the wet mixture into the dry ingredients. Stir just until mixed. *Do not overstir.*

5. Spoon the batter into a greased or papered muffin tin. Fill each cup nearly to the top.

6. Bake for 15 to 20 minutes.

7. Cool the muffins at least 10 minutes before removing from the tin.

8. When the muffins have cooled to room temperature, spoon about a teaspoon of the apricot preserves on each, smoothing it evenly on top. Sprinkle each with a large pinch of coconut.

NUTRITIONAL FACTS (per 96-gram muffin)
Calories: 202 (10% from fat)

Fat: 2 g	Cholesterol: <1 mg	Carbohydrates: 42 g
Protein: 4 g	Fiber: 2.8 g	Sodium: 207 mg
Potassium: 349 mg	Iron: 1.4 mg	Calcium: 74 mg

Tropical Fruit Muffins

I scoured the marketplace for the best dried fruits to create a tropical fruit muffin. Unexpectedly, I discovered an outstanding product in my regular grocery store. Packaged by Mariani Packing Company, Inc. in San Jose, California, Premium Tropical Medley contains pineapple, apricots, papaya, dark raisins, golden raisins, apples, and even coconut. Yet the chopped fruit conglomeration contains only one gram of fat per ounce.

I was so excited about this product's quality that I wrote to the Mariani Company and asked about their other products. To my delight, I learned that they package a full line of dried fruits. As luck would have it, I was able to find the products in a new grocery store in town. They are far and away the best dried fruits I have ever tasted.

In addition to being delicious, these high-carbohydrate, low-fat Tropical Fruit Muffins are energizing. Enjoy!

Dry Ingredients	Wet Ingredients
1¼ cups unbleached white flour	1 ripe banana, mashed (or ½ cup)
1 cup whole-wheat flour	1¼ cups skim milk
½ cup brown rice flour	½ cup honey
¼ cup light brown sugar	1 large egg
1½ teaspoons baking soda	1 tablespoon grated orange peel
1 teaspoon baking powder	2 teaspoons rum flavoring
¼ teaspoon sea salt	

Goodies

1 cup dried tropical fruit mix

Yield: 12 muffins

1. Preheat the oven to 400° F.

2. Sift the dry ingredients together in a large bowl.

3. Whisk the wet ingredients in a medium bowl or blend them in a food processor. Add the dried fruit and stir to combine.

4. Pour the wet mixture into the dry ingredients. Stir just until mixed. *Do not overstir.*

5. Spoon the batter into a greased or papered muffin tin. Fill each cup nearly to the top.

6. Bake for 15 to 20 minutes.

7. Cool the muffins at least 10 minutes before removing from the tin.

NUTRITIONAL FACTS (per 103-gram muffin)
Calories: 226 (5% from fat)

Fat: 2 g	Cholesterol: 20 mg	Carbohydrates: 51 g
Protein: 5 g	Fiber: 2.1 g	Sodium: 267 mg
Potassium: 314 mg	Iron: 1.5 mg	Calcium: 83 mg

Wantana's Thai Custard Muffins

I met Wantana during my second trip to the Buddhist monastery in England. We had both signed on to serve the monks and nuns during their two-month winter retreat. A slight Thai women, she stands only about 4 feet 8 inches tall but has more energy than three people twice her size. She brims with love and a genuine eagerness to be of service. I affectionately call her Mighty Mouse.

Each Friday evening, Wantana and her friend Chonlada arrived at the monastery with shopping bags filled with the ingredients needed to prepare their favorite Thai dishes. My favorite dish—Thai custard—is a specialty of Wantana's. In honor of their namesake, I always try to make Wantana's Thai Custard Muffins with as much love, generosity, and high spirit that I can.

Dry Ingredients	Wet Ingredients
1 cup whole-wheat pastry flour	1½ cups homemade coconut milk*
1 cup unbleached white flour	¾ cup nonfat sour cream
½ cup whole-wheat flour	2 large egg whites
¾ cup light brown sugar	1 teaspoon vanilla extract
2 teaspoons baking powder	
1 teaspoon baking soda	
¼ teaspoon sea salt	

Custard Sauce	Goodies
1 tablespoon light margarine	½ cup flaked coconut
1½ tablespoons cornstarch	
¾ cup skim milk	
3 tablespoons light brown sugar	
1 teaspoon vanilla extract	

* To make 1½ cups homemade coconut milk, combine ¼ cup grated coconut with 1¼ cups skim milk in a saucepan. Bring to a boil, lower the heat, and simmer for 3 minutes. Place the mixture in a blender on high speed for about 1 minute. Cool to room temperature.

Yield: 12 muffins

1. Preheat the oven to 400° F.

2. Sift the dry ingredients together in a large bowl.

3. Whisk the wet ingredients in a medium bowl or blend them in a food processor. Pour the wet ingredients into the dry ingredients. Stir just until mixed. *Do not overstir.*

4. Spoon the batter into a greased or papered muffin tin. Fill each cup nearly to the top.

5. Bake for 15 to 20 minutes.

6. While the muffins bake, prepare the custard sauce. Melt the margarine in a small saucepan over medium heat. Add the cornstarch and stir to form a smooth paste. Add the milk and brown sugar and reduce the heat to low. Cook the mixture, stirring frequently, until it thickens (about 15 minutes). Remove from the heat, add the vanilla, and stir to a smooth custard consistency. Set aside to cool.

7. Cool the muffins at least 10 minutes before removing from the tin.

8. To serve, place each muffin in the center of individual serving dishes. Spoon approximately 1 tablespoon of custard sauce over the top of each muffin. Top with a large pinch of flaked coconut. Serve warm.

NUTRITIONAL FACTS (per 103-gram muffin)
Calories: 190 (12% from fat)

Fat: 3 g	Cholesterol: 1 mg	Carbohydrates: 38 g
Protein: 5 g	Fiber: 1.9 g	Sodium: 258 mg
Potassium: 255 mg	Iron: 1.3 mg	Calcium: 141 mg

QUICK REFERENCE GUIDE

The following guide alphabetically lists (in chapter order) all of the recipes found in *Gloria's Gourmet Low-Fat Muffins* along with their defining ingredients. It is provided to help you easily select a recipe that includes specific ingredients you may desire.

2. Fresh and Fruity, Sometimes Nutty, Anytime Muffins

The following muffins are made with fresh and/or dried fruit (and sometimes nuts). They are great at any time.

Apple Ginger Muffins. Fresh apples, applesauce, crystallized ginger, ground ginger.

Berry Berry Delicious Muffins. Dried raspberries, dried cranberries, apple juice, nonfat sour cream.

Better Banana (Nut) Bran Muffins. Ripe bananas, wheat bran, roasted walnuts (optional).

Black Cherry Blossom Muffins. Dark sweet cherries, applesauce, lemon peel.

Blueberries, Oats, and Cream Muffins. Fresh blueberries, rolled oats, oat bran, nonfat sour cream, lemon peel.

Buckwheat Buttermilk Muffins with Blueberries and Maple Syrup. Buckwheat, nonfat buttermilk, fresh blueberries, maple syrup.

Catherine's Lemon Red Raspberry Muffins. Fresh raspberries, applesauce, nonfat buttermilk, lemon peel.

Cherry Irish Soda Muffins. Dark sweet cherries, orange peel, lemon peel, currants, caraway seeds, nonfat buttermilk. (Can also be made with dried cherries, cranberries, blueberries, or raspberries.)

Cranberry Apple Muffins. Dried cranberries, fresh apples, apple juice, nonfat buttermilk, orange peel, rum extract, cinnamon.

Friends of the Earth Vegan Muffins. Dates, dried fruit bits, roasted walnuts (optional), ripe bananas, nonfat soymilk, lemon peel, cinnamon, mace.

Lemon-Yogurt Poppy-Seed Muffins. Nonfat plain yogurt, lemon peel, poppy seeds.

Maple (Pecan) Muffins. Barley flour, malted milk powder, roasted pecans (optional), maple syrup.

Mom's Applesauce Muffins. Chunky applesauce, raisins, dates, cocoa powder, cinnamon, nutmeg, allspice.

Orange-Strawberry-Banana Muffins. Ripe bananas, orange peel, strawberry flavoring.

Pumpkin Banana Muffins. Pumpkin purée, ripe bananas, lemon peel, cinnamon, nutmeg.

3. Crunchy, Crumbly, Spicy Do-Da Muffins

The following muffins with their wonderful flavor and crunchy, crumbly toppings are just right with fresh-brewed coffee or tea.

Almond Cardamom Fig Muffins. Dried figs, sliced almonds, applesauce, ground cardamom seeds, almond extract. *Topping:* sliced almonds.

Almond Delight Muffins. Almonds, nonfat sour cream, almond extract, dark brown sugar. *Topping:* almonds, dark brown sugar.

Apple (Walnut) Crumble Muffins. Fresh apples, applesauce, nonfat buttermilk, roasted walnuts (optional). *Topping:* unbleached white flour, light brown sugar, cinnamon, light margarine.

Apple-iscious Apple Spice Muffins. Fresh apples, applesauce, apple butter, lemon peel. *Topping:* honey crunch wheat germ, light brown sugar.

Apricot Sesame Muffins. Canned apricots, dried apricots, nonfat buttermilk. *Topping:* sesame seeds.

Blueberries, Oats, and Cream Muffins, Too. Apple juice, fresh blueberries, malted milk powder, nonfat sour cream. *Topping:* unbleached white flour, whole-wheat flour, rolled oats, cinnamon, light brown sugar, light margarine.

Café Crumble Muffins. Fresh-brewed coffee, nonfat yogurt, honey, vanilla extract. *Topping:* unbleached white flour, whole-wheat flour, dark brown sugar, light margarine.

Coco Nana Muffins. Flaked coconut, ripe bananas, orange-juice concentrate, orange peel, rum flavoring. *Topping:* flaked coconut.

Crunchy Granola Crumble Muffins. Granola, applesauce, nonfat buttermilk, maple syrup. *Topping:* granola, whole-wheat flour, unbleached white flour, cinnamon, light margarine.

Double Ginger Ginger Muffins. Crystallized ginger, ground ginger, golden raisins, molasses, orange peel, cinnamon, nutmeg.

Girl Scout Date (and Nut) Muffins. Dates, roasted almonds (optional), flaked coconut, nonfat buttermilk, molasses, cinnamon, orange peel.

Jelly Crumb Muffins. All-fruit jelly, nonfat buttermilk. *Topping:* unbleached white flour, light brown sugar, cinnamon, light margarine.

Prune Spice Muffins. Prunes, nonfat buttermilk, roasted walnuts (optional), cinnamon, allspice, cloves.

Toasted Wheat Germ Crunch Muffins. Nonfat buttermilk, apple-juice concentrate, maple syrup. *Topping:* honey crunch wheat germ, light brown sugar, light margarine.

Wheat Berry Muffins with Dates. Cornmeal, rolled oats, wheat berries, applesauce, apple butter, dates, molasses. *Topping:* dark brown sugar, cinnamon.

4. Herby Cheesy Muffin Thangs

The following muffins are made with low-fat and no-fat cheeses, flavorful herbs, and a variety of other interesting thangs. They are perfect meal accompaniments.

Artichoke Hearts with Basil Muffins. Artichoke hearts, vegetable broth, Parmesan cheese, garlic, fresh basil.

Cottage Cheese with Pear Muffins. Nonfat cottage cheese, fresh or canned pears, honey, cardamom.

Crumbled Bleu with Pear Muffins. Bleu cheese, fresh or canned pears, nonfat buttermilk, honey.

French Onion Muffins. Onion, vegetable broth, nutritional yeast flakes, garlic, reduced-fat Swiss cheese, soy sauce, Dijon mustard, tarragon.

Garden Vegetable Cream Cheese Muffins. Fat-free cream cheese with garden vegetables, basil, sage, thyme, onion.

Kasha Muffins with Browned Onion. Kasha, onion, vegetable broth.

Lemon Cottage Dill Muffins. Fresh dill weed, nonfat cottage cheese, lemon peel.

Modified Mexicali Corn Muffins. Yellow cornmeal, nonfat buttermilk, jalapeño peppers, pimento, corn.

Oktoberfest Muffins. Rye flour, barley flour, malted milk powder, beer, reduced-fat Swiss cheese, caraway seeds.

Onion Corn Muffins. Yellow, white, or blue cornmeal, nonfat sour cream, onion, fresh parsley, white or yellow corn.

Pesto Muffins. Fresh basil, garlic, Parmesan cheese, walnuts, vegetable broth, nonfat buttermilk.

Potato Dill-Seed Muffins. Potato flakes, nonfat cottage cheese, vegetable broth, scallions, dill seed.

Ricotta Cheese with Basil and Rosemary Muffins. Rye flour, low-fat ricotta cheese, vegetable broth, fresh basil, fresh rosemary.

Roasted Red Pepper Muffins. Brown rice flour, fat-free garlic herb cream cheese, roasted red peppers, fresh rosemary.

Scarborough Fair Muffins. Rye flour, vegetable broth, nonfat buttermilk, parsley, sage, rosemary, thyme, honey.

Sun-Dried Tomato Corn Muffins with Cumin. Yellow or white cornmeal, sun-dried tomatoes, tomato juice, nonfat buttermilk, cumin seeds.

Tomato Basil Muffins. Sun-dried tomatoes, tomato sauce, garlic, fresh basil.

5. Chocolate Every-Which-Way-But-Fat Muffins

The following muffins are made with one form of chocolate or another. Need we say more?

Banana (Nut) Fudge Muffins. Ripe bananas, fresh-brewed coffee, milk chocolate, roasted walnuts (optional).

Chocolate Almond Muffins. Milk chocolate, cocoa powder, applesauce, sliced almonds.

Chocolate Cherry Muffins. Dark sweet cherries, cocoa powder, prunes.

Chocolate Chestnut Muffins. Milk chocolate, cocoa powder, nonfat sour cream, roasted chestnuts.

Chocolate-Chip Banana Muffins. Ripe bananas, semi-sweet chocolate.

Chocolate Ginger Muffins. Brown rice flour, cocoa powder, crystallized ginger, nonfat buttermilk.

Chocolate Mint Muffins. Fresh mint, cocoa powder, prunes.

Chocolate Raspberry Chambord Muffins. Fresh raspberries, semi-sweet chocolate, cocoa powder, nonfat buttermilk, raspberry liqueur.

Devil's Food Muffins with Nonfat Cream-Cheese Icing. Chocolate syrup, cocoa powder, nonfat buttermilk. *Icing:* nonfat cream cheese, powdered sugar, vanilla extract.

Double Chocolate Chocolate Muffins. Cocoa powder, milk chocolate, apple-juice concentrate, nonfat buttermilk.

Marvelous Marbled Muffins with Coffee Yogurt-Cheese Icing. Semi-sweet chocolate, cocoa powder, nonfat buttermilk. *Icing:* coffee yogurt cheese, powdered sugar.

Orange Chocolate Muffins. Semi-sweet chocolate, orange peel, orange-juice concentrate.

Pumpkin Chocolate-Chip Muffins. Pumpkin purée, semi-sweet chocolate, roasted walnuts (optional), cinnamon, nutmeg, allspice, cloves.

Roger's Chocolate Fruit-and-Nut Muffins. Cocoa powder, chocolate syrup, raisins, roasted walnuts, nonfat sour cream, orange peel.

White Chocolate with Raspberry Muffins. White chocolate, fresh raspberries, nonfat sour cream.

6. Over-the-Top and Out-of-the-Question Muffins

The following muffins are made with unusual or exotic ingredients. Many have interesting glazes or toppings.

Amaretto Muffins. Barley flour, dark sweet cherries, nonfat buttermilk, amaretto flavoring. *Topping:* sliced almonds, pearl sugar.

Bananas Foster Muffins. Ripe bananas, nonfat sour cream, brandy flavoring. *Topping:* honey crunch wheat germ.

Blueberry Peach-Schnapps Muffins. Oat bran, fresh blueberries, canned peaches. *Glaze:* peach schnapps, sugar, light margarine.

Butterscotch Pecan Muffins. Roasted pecans, fat-free butterscotch syrup, nonfat sour cream.

Caribbean Sweet-Potato Gingerbread Muffins. Sweet potato purée, fresh ginger root, molasses, orange peel, cinnamon, cloves, nutmeg.

Far East Muffins. Nonfat vanilla yogurt, fresh ginger root, cardamom, cinnamon, clove.

Flipped Apple Muffins. Applesauce, oat bran, rum flavoring.

Gingerbread Muffins with Lemon Curd Filling. Ground ginger, fresh ginger root, nonfat buttermilk, orange peel, lemon curd, ginger, cinnamon, nutmeg.

Grand Marnier Creamsicle Muffins. Brown rice flour, orange-juice concentrate, orange peel, nonfat sour cream. *Glaze:* Grand Marnier liqueur, sugar, light margarine.

Hillsborough House Inn Breakfast Muffins. Sweet potato purée, currants, dark brown sugar, molasses, cinnamon, cloves, nutmeg. *Topping:* roasted walnuts, honey crunch wheat germ, dark brown sugar, light margarine.

Mango with Crystallized Ginger Muffins. Fresh or canned mango, crystallized ginger, rum flavoring.

Patty's Reincarnated Cappuccino Muffins. Fresh-brewed coffee, cocoa powder, nonfat sour cream, cinnamon.

Pineapple Carrot Ginger Muffins. Dried pineapple, fresh carrots, fresh ginger root, apple-juice concentrate.

Pineapple Upside-Down Muffins. Crushed pineapple, applesauce, nonfat buttermilk.

Pistachio and Dried Cranberry Muffins. Dried cranberries, apple-juice concentrate, nonfat sour cream. *Topping:* pistachios, egg white.

Rum Raisin Muffins. Golden raisins, applesauce, low-fat vanilla yogurt, rum flavoring, nutmeg, cardamom.

Standard Spice Muffins with Vanilla Yogurt-Cheese Icing. Applesauce, nonfat buttermilk, golden raisins, dark brown sugar, cinnamon, nutmeg, ground ginger. *Icing:* yogurt cheese, vanilla extract, powdered sugar.

Sugar Plum Fairy Muffins. Brown rice flour, orange peel, lemon peel, applesauce, nonfat sour cream. *Glaze:* plum preserves, pearl sugar, cornstarch.

Triple-Apricot Ambrosia Muffins. Canned apricots, dried apricots, orange peel, coconut. *Topping:* apricot preserves, flaked coconut.

Tropical Fruit Muffins. Brown rice flour, dried tropical fruit mix (pineapple, apricots, papaya, dark raisins, golden raisins, apples, coconut), fresh bananas, orange peel, rum flavoring.

Wantana's Thai Custard Muffins. Flaked coconut, nonfat sour cream, onion. *Topping:* vanilla custard sauce.

INDEX